F-14 TOMC[AT]

HERMAN J. SIXMA &
THEO W. VAN GEFFEN

PLYMOUTH PRESS

IAN ALLAN
Publishing

Front cover:
F/A-18C/D
The F/A-18C/D Hornet is in use with the US Navy and Marine Corps along with the air forces of Canada, Australia, Spain, Finland and Switzerland. Northrop Grumman builds about 40% of the aircraft. As principal subcontractor to prime contractor McDonnell Douglas, Northrop has delivered well over a thousand aircraft.
Northrop Grumman Corporation, via The Aviation Picture Library

Back cover:
F-14
The contract to build the F-14 was awarded to Grumman in January 1969. Testing of the first prototype F-14A began in December 1970. The latest version, the F-14D began carrier operations in 1993.
Austin J. Brown/The Aviation Picture Library

Previous page:
F-14A, CAW-6 USS Forrestal
In full afterburner this F-14A Tomcat belonging to Carrier Air Wing 6 (CAW-6) takes off from one of USS *Forrestal's* two bow catapults. The ball of fire behind the aircraft denotes loss of fuel. This dramatic photograph was taken in latre January 1990 when Forrestal was sailing in the Mediterranean off Scicily, while participating in an anti-submarine warfare exercise.
Theo W. van Geffen, IAAP

First published 1989 — *F16 Fighting Falcon*
First published 1990 — *F15 Eagle*
First published 1991 — *F14 Tomcat*
First published 1993 — *F18 Hornet*
Combined edition 1998

ISBN — Ian Allan Publishing edition   0 7110 2568 X
ISBN — Plymouth Press edition   1 882663 25 X

© Ian Allan Publishing Ltd 1998

Published by Ian Allan Publishing

an imprint of Ian Allan Publishing Ltd, Terminal House, Station Approach, Shepperton, Surrey TW17 8AS.
Printed by Ian Allan Printing Ltd, Riverdene, Molesey Road, Hersham, Surrey, KT12 4RG.

PREFACE

To prepare a comprehensive colour album on the 'world's best total fighter', as Cdr Mike Denkler of VF-31 'Tomcatters' puts it when he refers to the F-14, is not an easy job.

First of all, compared to such star performers as the F-16 Fighting Falcon and the F-4 Phantom, the F-14 Tomcat is not one of the great export success stories for the US aircraft industry. Apart from 80 F-14s delivered to the (then) Imperial Iranian Air Force (IIAF), the US Navy is the only other customer for the aircraft.

Secondly, aircraft in service with the USN today are not as colourful as their forebears in the 1960s and 70s.

The first fact means this album is dedicated almost exclusively to USN Tomcats — except, of course, for a F-14 in IIAF colours. To overcome the problems of fact two we decided to include a number of pictures of the Tomcat from the 1960s and 70s when it was much more fun to look at — and bearing so many colourful reference points for autofocus (AF) cameras compared with today's low-visibility schemes which pose so many problems for AF cameras!

But problems apart, we believe we have succeeded in our task! So we should like to thank the following individuals and organisations for their indispensable help in the preparation of this album: Ens Lydia Zeller (Chinfo), Lt-Cdr Gene Okamoto (Point Mugu), NAS Miramar, Chief Howard (AIRPAC), Lt Jim Fallin, USS *Forrestal*, Cdr Dottie Schmidt (US Navy Reserve), Lois Lovisolo (Grumman Corporation), Don Spering (AIR), Frank B. Mormillo, J. Dennis Calvert, Robbie Shaw, Peter Foster and NASA.

Herman J. Sixma (IAAP)
Theo W. van Geffen (IAAP)
Amersfoort, Holland
May 1991

Far left:
F-14A (Plus) (161601, NG-201), VF-24, USS Nimitz Crewchief and crewmembers prepare to launch this F-14 and the aircraft involved is one of the batch of 32 modified F-14As. The TCS (Television Camera Set), a closed circuit television system, can be seen mounted beneath the nose of the aircraft, photographed at NAS Miramar's ramp on 1 May 1990.
Theo W. van Geffen, IAAP

Left:
F-14A (158616), NATC, NAS Patuxent River, Md This aircraft later replaced pre-production No 10 which crashed into Chesapeake Bay on 30 June 1972. Dedicated for carrier suitability, 158616 made its first flight on 23 October 1972 and was photographed on 20 March 1973 at NAS Patuxent River, Md. In 1981 the aircraft was in temporary storage before delivery to VF-201 at NAS Dallas, Tx, in early 1988.
Dr J. G. Handelman

F-14 TOMCAT

Right:
**F-14A (160401, AJ-101),
VF-41, USS Nimitz
Each CAW is equipped with a
squadron of all-weather A-6
Intruder fighter-bombers,
comprising A-6Es and up to
four KA-6Ds for in-flight
refuelling. Here a KA-6D of
VA-35 'Black Panthers' is
refuelling two F-14As of
VF-41. The 'AJ' code on the
Tomcats is visible on the
bottom of the rudder. Since
this picture was taken, CAW-8
transferred to CVN-71, USS
Theodore Roosevelt. In
response to the Iraqi invasion
of Kuwait in August 1990, the
carrier was one of three
ordered to join carriers in the
Gulf area .**
Grumman Corporation

The primary reason behind the development of the Grumman F-14 Tomcat lay in the cancellation of F-111B funds by US Congress in May 1968 and their subsequent transfer to the VFX-project. In the early 1960s, with the conservation of R & D funds in mind, Defense Secretary Robert McNamara recommended — and later insisted — that the US Navy (USN) and US Air Force (USAF) should combine their two missions of fleet air defence and nuclear strike in one aircraft. The Navy was very unhappy with McNamara's idea, arguing that its fleet air defence requirements were not at all compatible with the aircraft type required by the Air Force. However, on 1 September 1961, DoD gave the formal go-ahead to what was called the joint USAF/USN tactical fighter programme (TFX).

The TFX contest was won by General Dynamics on 26 November 1962 with its Model 12, contracts being placed for the F-111A (USAF) and the F-111B (USN), the latter variant being built by Grumman. The first flight of the F-111B took place on 18 May 1965 from Calverton, NY, but it soon became apparent that the F-111B was facing serious problems — pilots complained that because of the angle of attack, they were unable to see the carrier deck on approach. But the biggest threat to the programme was the weight of the aircraft: the carrier could not handle the 70,000lb of the first F-111B, which exceeded the USN requirement by 40%. Problems did not stop there, although Weight Improvement Programmes succeeded in reducing the aircraft's gross weight. In the meanwhile, Grumman had received some funds from the Navy for an advanced fighter study and in October 1967 the company proposed a way of wrapping a new airframe around the existing F-111B (TF30) engines and AWG-9 Weapons System. Extensive use of advanced materials such as titanium and boron so decreased the gross weight of the aircraft that the Navy became impressed with the superior performance of what had now become known as the VFX. On 17 December 1968 DoD announced Grumman and McDonnell-Douglas as the two finalists out of five competitors in the VFX competition. One month later the contract was awarded to Grumman.

Since production of the F-11 Tiger in 1958, Grumman had been out of the fighter business, but the experience with the variable geometry XF-10F Jaguar had given Grumman probably more knowledge about swing-wing technology than any other aircraft company. Since 1966, when VFX preliminary studies and pre-concept formulation work had commenced, Grumman engineers performed some 9,000hrs of wind tunnel tests on nearly 400 different combinations of engine air inlets and exhaust nozzles. These studies boiled down to eight specific design numbers: 303-60, 303A to G. The initial design 303-60 evolved into the award-winning 303E — a high wing variable-sweep airplane with potted engines. A second vertical fin was added to ensure directional stability. The F-14 Tomcat was born.

The three-phased programme of weapon system development would assure ever-increasing performance as advanced technology engines and avionics became available: the F-14B introducing an engine with major improvements in thrust and weight; the F-14C carrying advanced multi-mission avionics, with the F-14B engine/airframe combination remaining unchanged.

On 21 December 1970 testing commenced with the maiden flight of the prototype F-14A (157980). Nine days later this aircraft crashed, delaying flight testing until 24 May 1971, when the second F-14 took to the sky. (Altogether three F-14s were lost during these early test flights.) The arrival of the first F-14A at the Naval Missile Center in the autumn of 1971 marked the start of the integration testing of the F-14 and the AIM-54 Phoenix, a derivative of the two-stage Eagle missile originally planned to be carried by the F-6D Missileer. The first live firing in June 1972 meant the end of a QT-33 target. Initial carrier operating trials commenced on 15 June 1972, when an F-14A was catapulted from the USS *Forrestal* and deliveries of production Tomcats started in December 1972. On the 31st of that month VF-124, the fleet replacement training squadron at NAS Miramar, received its first aircraft. On 14 October 1972 a direct step was taken to prepare the F-14 for its operational use by commissioning VF-1 and VF-2 at NAS Miramar.

Note:

(1) In an administrative message the Chief of Naval Operations (CNO), Washington DC, ordered the redesignation of all F-14A (Plus) aircraft to F-14B as of 1 May 1991.

(2) Throughout this book we have used the acronym CAW for Carrier Air Wing rather than the military abbreviation CVW.

From F-14A to F-14D

Between December 1972 and the first months of 1987, when the last F-14A on order left the Grumman plant in Calverton, a total of 557 Tomcats were delivered. Most aircraft went to the USN. The only export customer for the F-14A was, and still is, Iran. In the period from January 1976 to July 1978 the, (then) Imperial Iranian Air Force (IIAF) took delivery of 80 F-14 Tomcats to counterbalance the threat of Soviet MiG-25s which frequently entered Iranian airspace. Besides the acceptance of the F-14A, Iran took an option on 70 F-14Bs, to be powered by the Pratt & Whitney F401 turbofan which would give the aircraft 30% more thrust than the original TF30-P-412A engine. However, the first attempt to get the 'Super Tomcat' into production failed due to budgetary restraints and the F401 engine was tested in only one aircraft (157986), which made its first flight on 12 September 1973. The F-14C remained a paper version only.

The introduction of a new generation of Soviet fighters (Su-27 'Flanker', MiG-29 'Fulcrum' and MiG-31 'Foxhound') convinced the USN in the early 1980s that its F-14A had not benefited from any threat-related improvements since its original introduction. To enable the Tomcat to engage the enemy at greater distances from the fleet, the aircraft's fuel efficiency and radar system had to be improved and its outdated analogue avionics needed to be replaced with modern digital technology. Rather than choosing to develop an entirely new aircraft, it was decided to upgrade the F-14A which would save $2-3 billion in development costs, and a new engine was already available. In earlier flight testing by Grumman, which started on 14 July 1981, the seventh production F-14A (157986) had been fitted with General Electric F101 Derivative Fighter Engines (DFE). The thrust increase was about 30 per cent, while fuel savings were significant. A standard F-14A was test-flown under the same conditions and at the end of each flight it had about one ton less fuel remaining in its tanks than the re-engined Tomcat. The F101 DFE was redesignated F110, and in February 1984 it was selected for installation in Tomcats to be ordered in Fiscal Year (FY) 87 and subsequent years, thus becoming step one in the two-step programme leading to the F-14D. The first flight of the re-engined F-14A — fitted with General Electric F110-6E-400 turbofan engines — took place from Calverton, NY, on 29 September 1986. Later testing included the digital avionics and improved radar for incorporation into the F-14D.

The first production F-14A (Plus) (162914) was accepted by the USN on 16 November 1987 and assigned to Naval Aircraft Test Center (NATC) at Patuxent River, Md, for flight-testing. The first operational F-14A (Plus) of a batch of 70 aircraft — 38 newly built and 32 modified F-14As — was assigned to VF-101, the East Coast fleet replacement training squadron, at NAS Oceana on 11 April 1988. By 1990 all F-14As (Plus) had been delivered. VF-142 and VF-143 were the first operational squadrons to be equipped with the Plus.

On 31 July 1984 an incrementally-funded fixed-price full-scale development (FSD) contract was signed for the design, development and qualification of an F-14D (and an F-14A (Plus)). 'In order to double the effectiveness of the F-14A weapons system against the advanced threat of the nineties and beyond', as the Naval Air Systems Command put it, the Hughes AWG-9 radar would be replaced by a Hughes APG-71 offering high-speed digital processing combined with improved target detection and tracking in a hostile electronic countermeasures environment. The programme would also include a Hughes/ITT joint tactical information distribution system (JTIDS) and an infra-red search and track system (IRSTS). A second contract called for the modification of six existing F-14As to the 'D' standard to flight-test the engines, radar equipment and avionics, and the production of 37 brand new aircraft. Altogether USN plans call for the production of a total of 127 new F-14Ds, while converting 373 F-14A/A (Plus) to the 'D' configuration. The Navy Air Rework Facility (NARF) at NAS Norfolk, Va, was contracted to convert two aircraft, while Grumman — competing primarily against the USN for more business — would convert four F-14s. The first test flight of the F-14D was conducted at Grumman's Calverton test flight facility on 23 November 1987.

Before the first production F-14D could be rolled out on 23 March 1990, Grumman and the USN had to counter a proposal by senior officials in the Office of the Secretary of Defense to kill the F-14D in FY90, because they thought that the low annual quantities and high unit costs ($73 million) would be an inefficient use of Navy funds. Without the production of new F-14Ds — rolling off the F-14 production line and ending the Tomcat 21 option — the USN would encounter inventory shortfalls commencing in FY93, forcing it to retire an F-14 Wing at expected attrition rates of 10 F-14s per year. Grumman would be forced to cut back employment even further than the 3,100 employees already announced for 1989. The USN's compromise plan to keep the production of new aircraft going made it, and in November 1989 President Bush signed the FY90 DoD budget, including the production of 18 new F-14Ds. However, DoD's FY91 budget request contains funds only to continue the modification of F-14As to F-14Ds, thus cancelling the production of further new F-14Ds. On 30 March 1990, the first production F-14D was flown to NATC for carrier suitability tests, followed by assignment to the Pacific Missile Test Center at NAS Point Mugu. The number 7 and 8 production F-14Ds arrived with VF-124 at NAS Miramar on 5 October 1990, while the formal acceptance took place on 16 November 1990. VF-51 and VF-111 are slated to become the first operational Tomcat units to convert to the D model in mid-spring 1991, while carrier deployment is scheduled for 1993.

Tomcat 21, the next generation?

The major aircraft review by the DoD in April 1990 resulted in the decision to postpone production of the Navy Advanced Tactical Fighter (N/ATF) by two years, until FY96. Any gap in the capability posed by a delay in the N/ATF programme could be countered by structural modifications to existing F-14s. The USN is doubting this and will request additional new F-14Ds as an interim solution in case the N/ATF is further delayed. Another possibility is the intro-duction of the Tomcat 21, an advanced F-14D Tomcat, which Grumman likes to offer to the Navy as an alternative to the ATF.

The Tomcat 21 is a Grumman proposal from 1988, including technology to reduce the Tomcat's radar signature, upgraded avionics and modifications to give the aircraft a ground-attack capability. Although the wiring to carry iron bombs is present in the F-14A, this capability has never been fully exploited. In late 1989, the F-14 and F-14A (Plus) were involved in a test programme from the NATC, aiming at giving the Tomcat an air-to-ground capability against various targets, using Mk 80 series bombs. Like the F-14D, development costs for the Tomcat 21 will be less than $1 billion. A first flight could take place by 1994.

A commitment to the N/ATF programme must be made before Grumman is forced to close the F-14 production line in 1992. In case the USN does not choose the ATF, the Tomcat 21 would not be viable without an on-going F-14D production because restart-ing the Tomcat production line would take some five years.

With the USN still committed to working with the USAF in the ATF-programme, prospects for the Tomcat 21 are not too good. However, with the TFX history in mind, building a Navy version of an aircraft primarily designed for the USAF is not the easiest way of procuring a new fleet air superiority fighter, but we may all be pleasantly surprised. Only time will tell.

Below left:
F-14A (TARPS) (160925, NJ-440, VF124, NAS Miramar, Ca
VF-124 Tomcats participated in RAM-86, the Reconnaissance Air Meet hosted by the 67th TRW at Bergstrom AFB, Tx, where 16 teams took part. The aircraft — equipped with TARPS — had been painted above the centreline with water-based camouflage paint.

In 1970, VF-124 was designated to help support a cadre of officers responsible for introducing the new F-14 aircraft to the fleet. Subsequently 'Crusader College' — F-8 training unit — transferred to VFP-63 in August 1972. The West Coast F-14 fleet replacement squadron thus became the first unit to convert to the Tomcat. With the arrival of F-14A 158620 on 31 December 1972, the delivery of Tomcats to the Gunfighters began.

On 6 March 1984 VF-124 became the first F-14 squadron to achieve 35,000 mishap-free flight hours. This is exceptionally noteworthy because the majority of flights are flown by newly-qualified aircrew with minimal type experience.
Don Spering, AIR

Right:

**F-14A (162592, NE-113),
VF-1, USS Ranger**
**Fighter Squadron One (VF-1)
was the first fleet fighter
squadron to become
operational on the F-14. Its
first Tomcat arrived on 1 July
1973 and a full complement of
12 aircraft was reached in
March 1974. The F-14
pictured has just launched an
AIM-54C Phoenix air-to-air
missile. The AIM-54C does not
require external cooling
systems at each mounting
station (a maximum of six
missiles can be carried) for
proper functioning in
comparison to the AIM-54A,
which does. The missile also
has about a one-third longer
range and improved
resistance to electronic
jamming. VX-4 at NAS Point
Mugu is still tasked with the
operational testing of the
Phoenix under various threat
conditions.**
US Navy, Lt-Cdr Art Legare

Above:

F-14A (159439, AE-204), VF-142, USS America
Mere seconds before its launch from USS *America* in the
Mediterranean off Crete, this VF-142 Tomcat is crouching — nose
down — on the No 3 catapult.

In October 1963 VF-193 was redesignated VF-142. The
'Ghostriders' conducted the first retaliatory strikes against North
Vietnam in August 1964. Conversion from the F-4B to the F-4J was
made in 1969 and in November 1970 VF-142 received the first
VF-121 'FATHA' Award, which goes to the F-4 squadron adjudged to
be the most outstanding in the US Navy. VF-142's Tomcat 159437
was the first production F-14 to achieve 1,000 flying hours on
8 February 1978.

On 24 May 1989 VF-142 became the first operational East Coast
F-14 squadron to receive the F-14A (Plus).

Theo W. van Geffen, IAAP

F-14A (161597, NH-200), VF-213
A scene on the washrack at NAS Miramar, Ca, on 30 April 1990.
Squadron commanders have the option to select up to two aircraft
in their unit for a full-colour paint scheme. The 'Black Lions' CO
decided to take this option and besides NH-200, NH-201 has a full-
colour paint scheme.
Theo W. van Geffen, IAAP

Above and overleaf:
F-14A (159831, XF-45), VX-4, NAS Point Mugu, Ca
F-14A (159853), VX-4, NAS Point Mugu, Ca
Air Test and Evaluation Squadron Four (VX-4) is stationed at NAS
Point Mugu, Ca, and was commissioned in 1952 as Air Development
Squadron Four. Its mission is to develop the best ways to use a
fighter aircraft and its weapons in the everyday operational
environment. It also includes the evaluation of F-14 Tomcat tactics
and operational procedures. VX-4 has been tasked with the
operational testing of the F-14D and is still testing the Phoenix
operationally under various threat conditions.
Theo W. van Geffen, IAAP

Right:

F-14A (159853), VX-4, NAS Point Mugu, Ca

VX-4 was the last active Navy squadron to fly the F-4 Phantom operationally. In 1969 one of the unit's F-4s was painted with a black anti-corrosive paint in an effort to determine the visibility of certain colours under various light conditions. Not until May 1971 was it suggested that the white bunny head on the tail would be an eye-catching emblem. (It was discovered rather quickly that black is no deterrent to corrosion, nor does it add to the plane's visibility.) When the final F-4S was lost in January 1990 it was decided to paint one of the unit's Tomcats in the black paint scheme, seen here on 2 May 1990.

Theo W van Geffen, IAAP

F-14A (160919, AB-210), VF-32, USS John F. Kennedy
Loaded with the maximum of six AIM-54 Phoenix air-to-air missiles, this 'Swordsmen' Tomcat is flying near its home station of NAS Oceana, Virginia. The AIM-54A requires external cooling systems at each mounting station for proper functioning.
Grumman Corporation

Previous page and right:
F-14A (159856, NL-106), VF-51, USS Carl Vinson
F-14A, VF-111, USS Carl Vinson
These photographs were taken in November 1985 while conducting carrier qualification trials aboard USS *Carl Vinson*. VF-51 aircrews conduct 'hot switch' crew exchanges so that the maximum number of flyers can be qualified in the shortest period of time.

VF-111 'Sundowners' made a total of seven Vietnam combat cruises, flying over 12,500 missions in SE Asia. The squadron began training for transition to the Tomcat in October 1977, which was completed in April 1978.

On 26 March 1984 VF-111's F-14A 160666 passed the one million flying hours for the Tomcat.
Frank B. Mormillo

Right:
F-14A (160669, NL-105), VF-51, USS Carl Vinson
VF-51 is the oldest fighter squadron to see continuous service in the Pacific Fleet. Equipped with F-8Es in the initial air-to-ground attacks against North Vietnamese PT boats and their bases after the Tonkin Gulf incident in August 1964, VF-51 converted to the F-14A in June 1978. The 1987/88 deployment aboard the *Vinson* included pioneering carrier operations in the freezing Bering Sea in the dead of winter. With its sister squadron, VF-111, it is assigned to CAW-15 aboard USS *Carl Vinson*, which deployed to the Western Pacific and Indian Ocean on 1 February 1990. After return from this deployment the carrier went into a two-year comprehensive overhaul.
Frank B. Mormillo

Right and far right:
**F-14A (158980, ND-204),
VF-302, NAS Miramar, Ca
F-14A (158997, ND 110),
VF-301, NAS Miramar, Ca**
VF-301 and 302 are both USN
Reserve squadrons at NAS
Miramar, Ca, assigned to
Carrier Air Wing Reserve 30
(CVWR-30). USNR units carry
out annual training
deployments aboard carriers
for carrier qualification
cruises.

VF-301 'Devil's Disciples'
was commissioned at Miramar
on 1 October 1970 during the
initial reorganisation of the
naval reserve force squadrons
and equipped with the F-8J
Crusader. It transitioned to
the F-14A on 11 October 1984
as the first USNR fighter
squadron. The conversion
ended 10 years of relationship
with the F-4 loosing their final
F-4s in late September 1984.
In March 1987 VF-301 took
part in an AIM-54A Phoenix
missile launch at PMTC. This
was the first use of a Phoenix
by a Naval Air Reserve
Squadron. In late 1989 VF-301
had accumulated 61,625
accident free hours in 19
years.

The 'Stallions' of VF-302
were commissioned on
21 May 1971 as the second
fighter unit in CVWR-30. In
1976 they were declared the
Battle 'E' as the best fighter
squadron in the USNR.
Theo W. van Geffen, IAAP

Left and below:
F-14A (159441, AE-104), VF-143, USS America.
F-14A (159440, AE-204), VF-142, USS America
In September 1973 VF-142 and 143 flew 12 F-4Js each to the American East Coast to begin carrier qualification trials aboard USS *America* **in preparation for their first peacetime cruise in 10 years. Returning to the USA and Miramar in August 1974 both units began transition to the F-14 Tomcat. On 1 April 1975, homeport was changed to NAS Oceana.**

The squadrons are presently assigned to CAW-7 aboard USS *Dwight D. Eisenhower,* **marking the first major deployment of the F-14A (Plus). The ship departed Norfolk, Va, for a routine deployment in the Mediterranean and also kept a close watch on the situation in Liberia.**

Theo W. van Geffen, IAAP

Right:
F-14A (160299, 3-863), IIAF
One of the F-14As for the
(then) Imperial Iranian Air
Force (IIAF) out of a batch of
80 aircraft can be seen here
in a pre-delivery flight near
Calverton, NY. The aircraft
were delivered between
January 1976 and July 1978.
The first contract for 30
Tomcats was signed in June
1974 and the second for 50 in
January 1975. Included in the
deal was the delivery of 424
Phoenix missiles, of which
only 270 were sent to Iran.

The Islamic revolution in
Iran brought an end to the
delivery of spare parts for the
F-14 (and subsequently
blocked the deliveries of 70
later model Tomcats, which
had already been paid for),
which led to a rapid
dismantling of the four F-14
squadrons at Shiraz and
Khatami. It is believed that at
the time of writing only a very
limited number of Tomcats —
but more than likely, none at
all — is still in service with the
Iranian Islamic Revolutionary
Air Force.
Grumman Corporation

Far right:
**A four-ship formation of
F-14As, of VF-201 overflies
downtown Dallas.**
US Navy

F-14 in the Gulf

The Tomcat played an important role in the Gulf — although it was not involved as spectacularly as the F-15 Eagle. F-14s accounted for only one kill, an Iraqi Mi-8 'Hip' helicopter which was hit by an AIM-9 from a VF-1 aircraft off USS *Ranger*.

USN participation in the Gulf started when the forward-deployed USS *Independence* (carrying CAW-14 with VF-21 and 154) and USS *Dwight D. Eisenhower* (carrying CAW-7 with VF-142 and 143) were dispatched from Seventh and Sixth Fleets respectively. The carrier battle groups provided ready air power to deter an Iraqi invasion of Saudi Arabia. Subsequently three more carriers were ordered to the Gulf: USS *Saratoga* (CAW-17 with VF-74 and 103), which sailed on 7 August to relieve the '*Ike*'; USS *John F. Kennedy* (CAW-3 with VF-14 and 32) on 15 August; and the USS *Midway* (no Tomcats assigned) from Yokosuka on 2 October to relieve *Independence*.

In December 1990 a further three carries went: on the 8th USS *Ranger* (CAW-2 with VF-1 and 2); and on the 28th USS *America* (CAW-1 with VF-33 and 102) and USS *Theodore Roosevelt* (CAW-8 with VF-41 and 84). At the start of 'Desert Storm' *America*, *Kennedy*, *Roosevelt* and *Saratoga* operated in the Red Sea, while *Midway* and *Ranger* were in the Persian Gulf.

The only F-14 loss of the war happened on 21 January when an F-14 (Plus) from USS *Saratoga* was downed by a SAM while on CAP over an Iraqi airfield. The pilot and RIO were listed as missing in action, but the next day one of them was recovered by a USAF special operations force.

On 25 February *John F. Kennedy* recorded its 10,000th arrested landing during deployment and its wing (No 3) had delivered over three million pounds of ordnance.

The Pentagon announced that CAW-9 and CAW-6 (on *Nimitz* and *Forrestal* respectively) would be deployed on 5 and 7 March: but events overtook them. The end of the war saw a scaling down of operations and a number of carriers left the Gulf — *Midway* to Yokosuka, *Saratoga* to Mayport, Fl, and *Kennedy* to Norfolk.

Since then *Theodore Roosevelt* has participated in Operation 'Provide Comfort', the humanitarian relief for the Kurds. *Both US Navy*

F-14A (161608, NK-203), VF-21, USS Constellation
Photographed at its home station NAS Miramar on 4 June 1986,
the F-14A of VF-21 is assigned to CAW-14 aboard USS
Constellation. However, on return from its most recent tour, the
squadron exchanged the 'Connie' for USS *Independence*, the
former going into SLEP, the latter leaving it . The 'Freelancers' and
its sister squadron the 'Black Knights' were the last fleet fighter
squadrons (Nos 9 and 10) at NAS Miramar to convert to the F-14.
The March 1985 deployment aboard USS *Constellation* was the first
ever deployment of a carrier with both F-14s and F/A-18s.
    The first two MiG-17 'kills' of the air war were claimed by F-8s of
VF-21 on 17 June 1965 while deployed aboard USS *Midway*. VF-21
'stood up' as an F-14 squadron on 15 March 1984, receiving its first
aircraft in December 1983, losing its last F-4N one month earlier.
US Navy, Michael Grove

F-14A, VF-31, USS Forrestal
Photographed in January 1990 off the coast of Sicily, this VF-31 Tomcat approaches the flightdeck of USS *Forrestal*. Landing an F-14 on the carrier is not an easy job. Although the landing speed of about 130kts is not very high, the wing area of the aircraft causes the wind to affect landing performance. Because the F-14 is a big aircraft, 1ft too high on the glidepath means a touchdown point which is 8m closer to the end of the flightdeck.
Herman J. Sixma, IAAP

Left and below:

F-14A (161860, AE-100), VF-11, USS Forrestal
F-14A (161864, AE-205), VF-31, USS Forrestal
The 'Red Rippers' and the 'Tomcatters', assigned to CAW-6 aboard
USS *Forrestal*, returned to Norfolk, Va, from a routine deployment
to the Mediterranean in April 1990. The Tomcats illustrated here
still carry full-colour unit markings, an exception to the Navy's
subdued colour schemes of today.

  To ease congestion on the flightdeck as well as to facilitate
hangar stowage, the wings of the F-14 can be placed in a 75°
'oversweep' position (the in-flight sweep ranges from 20° to 68°). A
central air data computer automatically moves the wings to the
optimum sweep angle for specific excess power (SEP) although,
when desired, the pilot can override the system and switch to
manual control. Maximum sweep rate is 7.5°/sec.

Herman J. Sixma, IAAP

F-14A (159444, AE-203), VF-32, USS Independence
CAW-3 is currently the parent Wing for VFs-14 and 32. Before being assigned to this Wing, the squadrons served with CAW-1 aboard USS *John F. Kennedy* and CAW-6 aboard USS *Independence*.
  CAW-3 is the second oldest Navy Air Wing, commissioned on 1 July 1938 aboard the first carrier to bear the name *Saratoga*. USS *John F. Kennedy* is the US Navy's largest non-nuclear carrier.
Robbie Shaw

Previous page and left:
F-14A (162689, AJ-101), VF-41, USS Theodore Roosevelt.
F-14A (161138, AJ-221), VF-84, USS Nimitz
VF-41, assigned to CAW-8, recently returned to the nuclear powered carrier, USS *Theodore Roosevelt*. The 'Black Aces' became the Navy's largest operational squadron in 1973 with 18 F-4Bs assigned, to evaluate a new concept in squadron organisation. December 1976 saw VF-41 converting to the F-14 Tomcat.

While on a routine mission over the Gulf of Sidra, two Tomcats of VF-41 were engaged by Libyan Su-22 'Fitters' which fired upon the F-14s with 'Atoll' air-to-air missiles. After evasion, both Su-22s were downed by AIM-9L Sidewinders. This action took place on 19 August 1981 while CAW-9 was deployed on the USS *Nimitz*.

The 'Jolly Rogers' operated the J B and N versions of the F-4 Phantom during four cruises aboard 'Rosey' (USS *Franklin D. Roosevelt*). The final F-4N was transferred in March 1976 and VF-84 began transition to the F-14 Tomcat.
Robbie Shaw
Dennis J. Calvert

F-14A (160392, AJ-210), VF-84, USS Nimitz
In most Carrier Air Wings, three F-14A (TARPS) aircraft have replaced the RA-5C Vigilante or RF-8G Crusader in the reconnaissance role. The tactical airborne reconnaissance pod system (TARPS) houses a CAI KS-87B frame camera for forward oblique or vertical photos, a Fairchild KA-99 panoramic camera and a Honeywell AAD-5 infra-red scanner. The TARPS is mounted under the rear fuselage and does not affect the number of missiles carried.
Grumman Corporation

F-14A (NE-201), VF-2, USS Kitty Hawk
With VF-1, the 'Bounty Hunters' belong to the first operational F-14
fleet squadrons. In 1982 VF-2 was designated a TARPS squadron,
and added airborne reconnaissance to their mission. In mid-1988
the squadron had logged 21,000 accident-free flying hours over a
five-year period.

The High Gunnery Trophy was presented in 1989 for the second
consecutive year to the 'Bounty Hunters'. The trophy is presented
to the F-14 squadron at Miramar which scores the highest
percentage of hits on the banner in a yearlong air-to-air gunnery
competition.
Frank B. Mormillo

F-14A (158984, NK-105), VF-1, USS Enterprise
VF-1 and VF-2 separated from VF-124, the F-14 Fleet Replacement
Squadron at NAS Miramar, and were commissioned on 14 October
1972, thus becoming the first operational fleet squadrons to be
equipped with the F-14A Tomcat. Both squadrons were assigned to
CAW-14 aboard USS Enterprise.
   Following completion of 'Project Up' which began in January 1974
to prepare for deployment, VF-1 and VF-2 commenced the first
Tomcat deployment on 17 September 1974 to the West Pacific and

Indian Ocean until 20 May 1975. During this deployment the units
flew protective aircover for the evacuation of refugees from Saigon
in 1975. The squadrons are presently assigned to CAW-2 aboard
USS Ranger.
Theo W. van Geffen, IAAP

Right:

F-14A (160906, AE-201), VF-32, USS Independence
Photographed at NAS Oceana on 10 October 1981 this colourful tail belongs to an F-14 of VF-32's 'Swordsmen'. The 'Swordsmen' of VF-32 became the Navy's first squadron to fly the F-9F Cougar in 1951 and the F-8 Crusader in 1956. In July 1974 the unit introduced the Tomcat to the East Coast and NAS Oceana after conversion training at NAS Miramar 18 March 1974 saw the arrival of their premier Tomcat. In October 1978 VF-32 completed nine years of accident-free flying hours with over 30,000 flown.
Theo W. van Geffen, IAAP

Above and overleaf:
F-14A (Plus) (163411, NG-212), VF-24, USS Nimitz
F-14A (Plus) (163410, NG-111), VF-211, USS Nimitz
**In 1975, VF-24 and VF-211 made their last Crusader cruise aboard
USS *Hancock* and upon return to San Diego transitioned to the F-14
Tomcat, VF-211 receiving its first aircraft on 1 December 1975 and
VF-24 eight days later.**

**NG-212's tail is adorned with the 'Boola, Boola' award. 'Boola,
Boola' is the radio transmission codeword given by a fighter crew
when they have scored a direct hit on a target. 'Boola, Boola' is also
an award, sponsored by Hughes Aircraft Company and presented to
the Pacific fighter squadron with best air-to-air missile readiness.
On 18 April 1990 this award was presented to 'The Fighting
Renegades'. During the grading period they converted to the F-14A
(Plus).**
Theo W. van Geffen, IAAP

Right:
F-14A (Plus) (163410, NG-111), VF-211, USS Nimitz
VF-211 and VF-24 recently converted to the more powerful F-14A (Plus), both receiving their first Plus on 14 April 1989. On 1 May 1990 when this photograph was taken at NAS Miramar, each of the units still had one straight F-14A left.
The 'Checkmates' of VF-211 won the highly coveted Admiral Joseph C. Clifton Award for 1984, recognising the squadron as the most outstanding fighter squadron in the US Navy.
Theo W. van Geffen, IAAP

Right:

F-14A (161857, AE-104)
VF-11, USS Forrestal
According to official Chief of Naval Operations' Records, VF-31 and 'Felix', its renowned Tomcat, have been together for 45 years, although recollections of 'old timers' indicate that 'Felix' is as old as 67 years.
In September 1974 the 'E' (capture of the Naval Air Force, Atlantic Fleet, Battle Efficiency Award) and 'S' (Aviation Safety Award) on the sides of VF-31s Phantoms were replaced by the large number One on both intakes when the 'Tomcatters' were awarded the Admiral Joseph C. Clifton Award as the outstanding fighter squadron in the Navy.
Theo W. van Geffen, IAAP

Far right:

F-14A (162600, NE-203),
VF-2, USS Ranger
This photograph taken in December 1987 depicts CAW-2 aircraft aboard USS *Ranger* (CV-61) during a port visit in the Western Pacific. NE-203 of 'The Bounty Hunters' sports an 'E' under the canopy, recognising the squadron as holder of the Pacific Fleet Naval Air Force Battle Efficiency Award.
Robbie Shaw

Right and far right:
F-14A, VF-202, NAS Dallas, Tx
F-14A (158635, AF-205), VF-202, NAS Dallas, Tx
USNR units carry out annual training deployments aboard active Navy carriers for carrier qualification. Here F-14s of VF-202, assigned to CVWR-20 at NAS Dallas, are launched from USS *America* off the Atlantic coast of the USA. With the conversion of VF-202, USNR F-14 acquisition was completed in 1988. Several of the Tomcats came from temporary storage, although the squadron received two brand new aircraft from the Grumman factory at Calverton, NY. VF-202's final F-4S left for storage at AMARC on 14 May 1988.

Conversion to the Tomcat for CVWR-20 had started with the arrival of the first one (assigned to VF-201) on 13 December 1986, although maintenance training had already commenced on 24 October with the arrival of 158634.
Don Spering, AIR

F-14A (161298, NH-100), VF-114, USS Enterprise
VF-114 'Aardvarks' was the first Pacific squadron to receive the F-4B Phantom. In August 1988 the unit was presented with the 'Mutha' Trophy for the third time, recognising the squadron as the best Pacific Fleet fighter squadron. In mid-1989 VF-114 had accumulated 18,600 accident-free hours over a five-year period. See inside of the left tail, expressing the emblem of CAW-11. This particular aircraft is the 'CAG bird'.
Theo W. van Geffen, IAAP

F-14A (Plus) (162919, AA-101), VF-74, USS Saratoga
Together with her sister squadron VF-103, VF-74 belongs to CAW-17 aboard USS *Saratoga*. The Air Wing is the second of the East Coast fighter squadrons equipped with the F-14A (Plus). Both units have a mixed complement of converted F-14As brought up to the Plus standard and brand new aircraft. After the escalation of tension in the Persian Gulf area during 1990 USS *Saratoga* with CAW-17 embarked was rushed to the area and joined USS *Dwight D. Eisenhower*, whose Air Wing includes the other two F-14A (Plus)-equipped fighter squadrons.
US Navy, VF-74

Below and right:
F-14A (160915, NH-212), VF-213
F-14A (159637, NH-100), VF-114, USS Lincoln
Carrier Air Wing 11's VF-114 and 213 returned to their homestation NAS Miramar on 16 March 1990 after a routine deployment aboard the USS *Enterprise* to the Western Pacific and the Indian Ocean. The time at home usually means training in preparation for the next deployment. This next deployment will not be made aboard USS *Enterprise* as the ship is undergoing a two-year comprehensive overhaul. After the transfer of the Navy's newest 'Nimitz' class aircraft carrier, USS *Abraham Lincoln*, to the Pacific Fleet in the autumn of 1990, CAW-11 exchanged the *Enterprise* for the *Lincoln*. When these photographs were taken at NAS Miramar on 1 May 1990, VF-213's Tomcats did not carry a carrier's name at all, while VF-114's Tomcats carried a mix of USS *Enterprise* and USS *Lincoln*, while the unit had two NH-100s, one with USS *Enterprise* and one with USS *Lincoln* on the tail . . .
Theo W. van Geffen, IAAP

Left and below:

F-14A (157991, 991), NASA, Edwards AFB, Ca
F-14A (158613, 834), NASA, Edwards AFB, Ca
In the late 1970s/early 1980s, several F-14A Tomcats were loaned
by the Naval Air Systems Command to NASA's Flight Test Research
Center at Edwards AFB, Ca. Included were the No 12 pre-
production F-14 (157991) and the No 2 production F-14 (158613),
which were flown in a joint NASA/USN research programme. With
two USAF F-15 fighters and the YF-17, the Tomcats were flown as
part of NASA's in-flight research on (then) current high-speed
military aircraft. Included in the F-14 programme was an in-flight
assessment of a new control system concept developed by NASA.
Data from the programme has been used to help in the design of
new high-speed aircraft.
NASA

Below and right:
F-14D (161867, 253), Grumman

F-14D 161867 is one of six original F-14As modified to the D
configuration. These aircraft are used to flight-test the engines,
radar equipment and avionics.

A new aircraft like the F-14D will go to the Naval Air Test Center
at NAS Patuxent River first for flight testing. After that it will move
to NAS Point Mugu on the West Coast for missile integration testing
with the Pacific Missile Test Center and for operational testing with
VX-4.

These photographs were taken at NAS Point Mugu on 2 May 1990
before and after the same mission. The aircraft left with an AIM-9
Sidewinder on a pylon under the left and right wing and with an
AIM-54 Phoenix under the left and right side of the fuselage. After
returning only the Sidewinder on the right side and the Phoenix on
the left side were left.

Theo W. van Geffen, IAAP

Right:

F-14A (NJ-451), VF-124, NAS Miramar

VF-124 on the West Coast and VF-101 on the East Coast are the two Navy F-14 Tomcat Replacement Squadrons.

Initially VF-124 carried out all F-14 instruction at NAS Miramar. To improve Atlantic Fleet readiness and to save time and money, it was decided to establish Tomcat training at NAS Oceana.

VF-124 is the Navy's Tomcat replacement squadron, which carries out the training of F-14D pilots and RIOs. On 5 October 1990 the unit received the first two F-14Ds, while the formal acceptance took place on 16 November 1990. The empty weight of the F-14A is 18,036kg, while its mission weight (including six AIM-54 Phoenix missiles) is 31,945kg. Max speed is around Mach 2.34, landing speed is 226km/h, and the minimum landing distance (without external aids) is 762m.

US Navy

Previous page, right and far right:
TA-3B (144867, 77), PMTC, NAS Point Mugu, Ca.
F-14A (160378,220), PMTC, NAS Point Mugu, Ca
The Pacific Missile Test Center (PMTC), originally established as the Naval Air Missile Test Center, at NAS Point Mugu, Ca, is at the forefront of developing and testing missile systems for the Fleet, making PMTC the Navy's primary facility for air-launched weapons. Other missions include fleet operations support and training. PMTC's Sea Test Range comprises a fully instrumented 35,000sq mile area, about 125 by 250 miles long.

To carry out its mission, PMTC flies all versions of the F-14 Tomcat and F/A-18 Hornet. Also assigned are EP-3A and RP-3A Orion aircraft, drone aircraft like QF-4 and QF-86. The PMTC A-3 Skywarriors with VAQ 33/34 ERA-3Bs probably are the only ones left in US Navy service, and are used as missile support aircraft. The TA-3B, photographed on 2 May 1990, is equipped with an F-14 nose, housing the Hughes APG-71 radar. This radar is similar to the APG-70 radar in the F-15 Eagle, and provides the aircraft with a six-fold improvement in data processing. The emblem on the TA-3's tail includes 'Hughes APG-71 radar'.
Theo W. van Geffen, IAAP

Right and far right:

F-14A (161435, AD-167), VF-101, NAS Oceana, Va

F-14A (161435, AD-167), VF-101, NAS Oceana, Va
Part of the pilot's and RIO's conversion training to the F-14 Tomcat includes carrier qualification in the type. Here we see VF-101's '167' in action aboard CV-66, USS *America* off the Atlantic coast in May 1988. The aircraft carries the 'S' on the tail, meaning that VF-101 had won the Aviation Safety Award. VF-101, the 'Grim Reapers', is the East Coast Replacement Squadron, stationed at NAS Oceana, Va. Its mission is to train replacement pilots, radar intercept officers (RIO), and enlisted maintenance personnel for Atlantic Fleet F-14 squadrons, and is the sole USN training unit for the F-14A (Plus).

After introducing the F-14 in January 1976, VF-101 kept the F-4 Phantom in its inventory until August 1977, when the squadron was split into two squadrons with the F-4 component and the Key West Detachment commissioned as VF-171, and the F-14 component continuing as VF-101.

On 11 April 1988 the 'Grim Reapers' received the first production F-14A (Plus) in the US Navy. Detachment Key West was revived on 27 June 1989 at NAS Key West, Fl, with up to 10 F-14s, primarily for ACM (Air Combat Manoeuvring) training.

Don Spering, AIR

Above and right:
F-14A (161621, NL-200), VF-111, USS Carl Vinson
F-14A (162594, NL-200), VF-111, USS Carl Vinson
The return on 29 July 1990 of the 'Sundowners' to NAS Miramar marked the end of the unit's deployment with the 'A' version of the Tomcat. In the mid-spring of 1991 VF-111, together with its sister squadron VF-51, was slated for conversion to the new F-14D Super Tomcat, while their first deployment aboard a carrier will take place in 1993.

**   While deployed, VF-111 participated in a Battle Group Evaluation, 'Team Spirit '90', Air Combat Manoeuvring with VC-5 in Cubi Point and exercises with the air forces of Singapore, Malaysia and Thailand. Altogether 'The Sundowners' accumulated over 2,200 flying hours and 1,000 arrested landings aboard USS *Carl Vinson*.**
US Navy, VF-111
US Navy, Lt Jim Ingalls

A KA-6D of Attack Squadron 52 refuels an Omani Jaguar while being escorted by a 'Sundowners' F-14A equipped with Sidewinder and Sparrow air-to-air missiles.
US Navy

F-14A (162597, NE-100), VF-1 USS Ranger
VF-1 was the first fleet fighter squadron to become operational on the F-14. Its first Tomcat arrived on 1 July 1973 and the full complement of 12 aircraft was reached in March 1974. The aircraft is armed with three types of air-to-air missiles: the AIM-54C Phoenix, which has about a one-third longer range than the AIM-54A and an improved resistance to electronic jamming, the AIM-7 Sparrow and an AIM-9M Sidewinder, both on the outboard wing pylon.
US Navy, Lt-Cdr Art Legare

F-14 TOMCAT UNITS

Home Station NAS Oceana, Va

Squadron/Nickname	Equipment	Converted from	CAW/Code	Carrier	Remarks
VF-11 Red Rippers	F-14A	F-4J	6/AE	USS Forrestal (CV-59)	
VF-14 Tophatters	F-14A	F4B	3/AC	USS John F. Kennedy (CV-67)	
VF-31 Tomcatters	F-14A (TARPS)	F-4J	6/AE	USS Forrestal (CV-59)	
VF-32 Swordsmen	F-14A (TARPS)	F-4B	3/AC	USS John F. Kennedy (CV-67)	
VF-33 Starfighters	F-14A	F-4J	1/AB	USS America (CV-66)	
VF-41 Black Aces	F-14A	F-4N	8/AJ	USS Theodore Roosevelt (CVN-71)	
VF-74 Be-devilers	F-14A (PLUS)	F-4S	17/AA	USS Saratoga (CV-60)	
VF-84 Jolly Rogers	F-14A (TARPS)	F-4N	8/AJ	USS Theodore Roosevelt (CVN-71)	
VF-101 Grim Reapers	F-14A/F-14A (Plus)	—	-/AD		Atlantic Training Sqn
VF-101 DetKey West	F-14A/F-14A (Plus)	—	-/AD		Est 27-6-89
VF-102 Diamond Backs	F-14A (TARPS)	F-4J	1/AB	USS America (CV-66)	
VF-103 Sluggers	F-14A (PLUS) (TARPS)	F-4S	17/AA	USS Saratoga (CV-60)	
VF-143 Ghostriders	F-14A (PLUS) (TARPS)	F-4J	7/AG	USS Dwight D. Eisenhower (CVN-69)	
VF-142 Pukin' Dogs	F-14A (PLUS)	F-4J	7/AG	USS Dwight D. Eisenhower (CVN-69)	

Home Station NAS Miramar, Ca

Squadron/Nickname	Equipment	Converted from	CAW/Code	Carrier	Remarks
VF-1 Wolfpack	F-14A	—	2/NE	USS Ranger (CV-61)	
VF-2 Bounty Hunters	F-14A (TARPS)	—	2/NE	USS Ranger (CV-61)	
VF-21 Freelancers	F-14A	F-4N	14/NK	USS Independence (CV-62)	From USS Constellation. PCS to NAS Atsugi 1991
VF-24 Fighting Renegades	F-14A (PLUS)	F-8J	9/NG	USS Nimitz (CVN-68)	
VF-51 Screaming Eagles	F-14A	F-4N	15/NL	USS Carl Vinson (CVN-70)	To convert to F-14D spring 1991
VF-111 Sundowners	F-14A (TARPS)	F-4N	15/NL	USS Carl Vinson (CVN-70)	To convert to F-14D spring 1991
VF-114 Aardvarks	F-14A	F-4J	11/NH	USS Abraham Lincoln (CVN-72)	From USS Enterprise
VF-124 Gunfighters	F-14A/F-14D	F-8J	-/NJ	—	Pacific Training Sqn. First F-14 received 5 Oct 1990
VF-154 Black Knights	F-14A (TARPS)	F-4N	14/NK	USS Independence (CV-62)	From USS Constellation. PCS to NAS Atsugi 1991
VF-191 Satan's Kittens	F-14A	—	10/NM	—	Est 4-12-86; dis 29-4-88
VF-194 Red Lightnings	F-14A (TARPS)	—	10/NM	—	Est 1-12-86; dis 29-4-88
VF-211 Checkmates	F-14A (PLUS) (TARPS)	F-8J	9/NG	USS Nimitz (CVN-68)	
VF-213 Black Lions	F-14A (TARPS)	F-4J	11/NH	USS Abraham Lincoln (CVN-72)	From USS Enterprise
VF-301 Devil's Disciples	F-14A	F-4S	30/ND	—	USN Reserve
VF-302 Stallions	F-14A (TARPS)	F-4S	30/ND	—	USN Reserve

Home Station NAS Dallas, Tx

Squadron/Nickname	Equipment	Converted from	CAW/ Code	Carrier	Remarks
VF-201 *Hunters*	F-14A	F-4S	20/AF	—	USN Reserve
VF-202 *Superheats*	F-14A (TARPS)	F-4S	20/AF	—	USN Reserve

Home Station NAS Point Mugu, Ca

Unit/Nickname	Equipment	Converted from	Code
PMTC/—	F-14A/F-14A (PLUS)/F-14D	—	—
VX-4 *Evaluators*	F-14A/F-14A (PLUS)/F-14D	—	XF

Home Station NAS Patuxent River, Md

Unit/Nickname	Equipment	Converted from	Code
NATC/-	F-14A/F-14A (PLUS)/F-14D	—	7T

Home Station NAS China Lake, Ca

Squadron/Nickname	Equipment	Converted from	Code
VX-5 *Vampires*	F-14A	F-14 reassigned	XE

F-14 PRODUCTION

F-14As modified as F-14A (Plus) — 32 aircraft

161287	161434
161416	161435
161417	161437
161418	161438
161419	161440
161421	161441
161422	161442
161424	161444
161425	161599
161426	161601
161427	161608
161428	161610
161429	161851
161430	161870
161432	161871
161433	161873

F-14A (Plus) new aircraft — 38 aircraft

Block 145	162910-162927	(18)
Block 150	163215-163229	(15)
Block 155	163407-163411	(5)

F-14As modified as F-14D — 18 aircraft

159600*	161134*	(=FY90)	**Grumman
610**	158**		*Navy Rework Facility
625**	159**		
159592**	161133**	(=FY91)	**Grumman
613**	135**		*Navy Rework Facility
619**	141**		
628*	145*		
629**	160**		
631*	166*		

F-14D new aircraft — 37 aircraft

FY88	163412-163418	(7)
FY89	163893-163904	(12)
FY90	164340-164351	(12)
	164599-164604	(6)

(No contracts for new F-14Ds after FY90)

F-14A, VF-24, USS Nimitz
With VF-24's conversion from the F-14A to the F-14A (Plus), to take photographs like this one is a thing of the past. The F-14A (Plus) simply does not need afterburners anymore for launching from a carrier. Its General Electric F110-400 engines give it a 30% thrust increase over the F-14A's Pratt & Whitney TF-30 engines, while they are much more fuel-efficient. The lack of the afterburner nozzle is the only external difference between the straight Tomcat and the Plus.
US Navy, VF-24

F-15 EAGLE

PETER R. FOSTER

Previous page:
Although the 48th FIS maintains an alert facility at Tyndall AFB, this pair of F-15As, 76-0113/104, climb out from the runway whilst representing the team during the 1982 'William Tell' competition. The 48th was the first ADC unit to receive the Eagle and at that time the unit insignia included the phrase 'Protectors of TAC'.
Peter R. Foster

PREFACE

No doubt the finest fighting machine within the Western inventory today, the McDonnell Douglas F-15 Eagle is hampered by only one real problem: cost! It therefore has met with relatively little export success and as such belongs to a very elite club.

The Eagle was conceived as the result of a two-year study, including two six-month studies by industry, to find a fighter replacement for the McDonnell Douglas F-4 Phantom in the counter-air threat role. The concept called for an aircraft that was capable of meeting the 'Beyond Visual Range' (BVR) intercept as well as having the ability to counter the close-air threat. Arising from this study came the 'F-X' fighter which ultimately became the F-15 Eagle that we know and respect so well today.

To incorporate all the necessary avionics as well as two Pratt & Whitney F100PW-100 turbofan engines – each developing 23,820lb of thrust and giving a combat thrust-to-weight ratio of 1.4:1 – and sufficient wing area to enable close combat manoeuvring, it was inevitable that such an aircraft would be big. The F-15 is certainly that but with **adept** colouring, a fire control system developed around an APG-63 and the most advanced weapon system available today, it is held in high esteem by air forces in both the East and West. Surprisingly, in respect of cost, it is now a cheaper aeroplane than the Panavia Tornado F3 and considered by many to be vastly superior. Having said that, the argument over single and two-man systems will continue forever, and therefore the suitability of each type is very much one of personal preference.

Service introduction of the Eagle began in November 1974 with the formation of the 555 TFTS 'Triple Nickle' at Luke AFB in Arizona to begin crew training for what was ultimately to become eight wings of air defence F-15s. Development and trials units were also given the opportunity to evaluate the F-15 in the intervening two years since the type's first flight on 27 July 1972.

To bring the F-15 Eagle into Tactical Air Command's (TAC) frontline inventory, the 56th Tactical Fighter Wing at McDill AFB was re-activated on the F-4 Phantom, taking over those jets previously assigned to the 1st TFW to release the Wing to re-form on the F-15 at Langley AFB, Virginia. Langley was and still is the headquarters of the Tactical Air Command and thus a fitting place for the Eagle's frontline service to begin.

However, with the US policy of keeping its frontline in both Europe and the Far East equipped with the most up-to-date equipment, the introduction of such a formidable type as the Eagle was inevitably only a short step away. As such, the second wing to equip on the type was the 36th TFW at Bitburg in West Germany in April 1977, but it was to be three more years before the type saw service in the Far East. This began following the introduction of the second major derivative which incorporated 2,000lb more internal fuel as well as provision for Fuel and Sensor Tactical Pack (FAST) pallets, and a programmable radar signal processor which enabled significant radar and avionic enhancements.

Export of the Eagle has been limited only to those countries favoured by the United States, and also those who can afford its large price tag. Israel received the aircraft from its 1976 fiscal budget and incorporated four reworked former USAF development aircraft within its purchase. It is here that the Eagle has been tested in combat, leading to its sale to the only other users, Saudi Arabia and Japan.

The airframe had by this time proved itself capable of being able to sustain significant updates to both weapon and avionic suits. Therefore the potential for such an aircraft has led to its introduction into roles not initially foreseen, and which will see its continued production ensured for many more years to come.

In the following pages I aim, through the lenses of some of the world's most notable photographers, to show the type's introduction into service and describe through the illustrations and captions the role and usage of this unique aeroplane.

Peter R. Foster
Brampton

The third development F-15A, 71-0282, was used in the avionics test phase. It is seen here at Edwards AFB in October 1977 in the markings of the USAF Flight Dynamics Laboratory Advanced Environmental Control System. *Peter R. Foster collection*

In the early flight development days the bulk of the prototype batch of Eagles displayed liberal amounts of dayglo. Here at Edwards AFB in June 1978 are 71-0288 and 71-0286, the latter of which has since passed into the technical training role at Chanute AFB, Illinois.
Frank B. Mormillo

Following on from the initial batch of 11 prototypes came a batch of eight pre-production machines. These, however, had a limited career with 72-0119 becoming the famous 'Streak Eagle' and subsequently has been preserved in the national collection at Wright Patterson AFB. Four other examples, 72-0116-8/20, were reworked to production standard and supplied to Israel in advance of its 1976 fiscal purchase. 72-0118 is seen here during Israeli crew training at Luke AFB in October 1975.
Peter R. Foster

Prior to 'Triple Nickle' – the 555th TFTS – coming on stream at Luke AFB, the initial operational development work was carried out by the 57th FWW. These operations began at Luke AFB prior to the unit establishing itself at Nellis with the Eagle. Here F-15As 73-0085/95 make a paired approach to Luke AFB in October 1975, and although displaying the Luke 'LA' tail code, they sport the 57th FWW checked fin band and unit insignia. *Peter R. Foster*

Although the Eagle was the ultimate outcome of the 'FX' study, much of the development work done by Boyd (insofar as combat manoeuvring) led to the development of the F-16 Fighting Falcon. Seen here ably displaying both types in service with the reserves are F-15A 73-0095 of 122nd TFS Louisiana ANG; and F-16As 79-0294/SC and 79-0295/SC of the South Carolina ANG. *Don Spering/AIR*

Far left:
The first examples of the Eagle began to be passed to the reserves in 1986 with the 122nd TFS Louisiana being one of the first recipients. Here seen climbing out of New Orleans NAS is F-15A 73-0096 which had previously served with 'Triple Nickle' at Luke AFB.
Don Spering/AIR

Left:
Never an easy shot, and one where you must have the camera set up prior to the manoeuvre, otherwise the 'g' force will prevent you lifting the same. These three Louisiana F-15s are caught high over the Gulf of Mexico in November 1986. *Don Spering/AIR*

Far left:
TF-15A as it was, 73-0108 arrived at Luke in 1975 suitably inscribed as 'TAC-1'. Not to be outdone here is 73-0112 doctored to represent the 12th AF commander's aircraft. In the late 'seventies much adding of high visibility marks went on, whilst at the same time elsewhere the search was on for the opposite. *Frank B. Mormillo*

Left:
The Reserves, as part of the USAF 'Total Force' concept, have to train in a similar fashion to the frontline units. In the event of hostilities they would in many cases deploy in advance of the Regulars, as was demonstrated during the South East Asia conflict. In this photograph a Louisiana ground-crew practice turning around and rearming an F-15 during NBC conditions.
Don Spering/AIR

In a period of around 10 years the 128th TFS Georgia ANG went through four changes of equipment. They were still operating the F-100D Super Sabre in 1975. From the 'Sled' they transitioned to the F-105G Thunderchief in a 'Wild Weasel' suppression role before receiving the F-4D Phantom. This last transition was perhaps the shortest, the unit receiving its first Eagles in 1986 at the same time as Louisiana. Here F-15A 74-0128 formates alongside F-4D 66-7605.   *Don Spering/AIR*

As stated earlier, whilst various high visibility schemes were appearing at Luke AFB, the search was also on for the opposite. Here F-15A 74-0110 displays a splinter air defence colour scheme that was not actually adopted: it was considered that hard lines were counter-productive.
Peter R. Foster collection

Far left:
The 21st CW at Elmendorf in Alaska was the last of the major commands to receive the Eagle, and then it was initially the early 'A' model only. Seen here climbing out of Nellis AFB during a 'Red Flag' exercise is one such example from the unit. *Frank B. Mormillo*

Above left:
Hawaii received the Eagle to replace its ageing F-4C Phantoms and was able to adopt the same attractive scheme that had previously been applied to both the F-4 and the F-102. F-15A 74-0135 is pictured taking off from Hickham's well used runway during mid-1988. *Ron Houghton*

Below left:
The 199th FIS in Hawaii received its early model F-15s from the re-equipping Alaskan squadrons. As the newer ex-USAFE 'C' models arrived at Elmendorf so too were batches of 74 fiscal 'As' delivered out to Hawaii. Some aircraft were, however, reassigned whilst at depot level maintenance which is conducted at Warner-Robins in Georgia. F-15A 74-0083 pictured at Hickham was one of the first aircraft to be assigned to the 1st TFW at Langley AFB in 1985. *Ron Houghton*

When Aerospace Defense Command (ADC) de-activated in 1982 and the Command became part of TAC, the F-15 Eagle was relatively quick to phase out the last real vestiges of the 'century' series fighters. The Eagles began re-equipping the 325th TTW in 1984 and eventually grew to three squadrons of early 'A' model aircraft. Formating on an Arkansas ANG KC-135A are four examples from the 2nd TFTS including 75-0041 marked as the wing commander's aircraft. *Don Spering/AIR*

The object of the 325th TTW at Tyndall AFB is to teach aircrew
progressing on to the Eagle the art of aerial intercepts and as such serves
as an interim between type conversion at Luke AFB and operational
work-up at squadron level. The unit also runs weapon instructor courses
and hosts the biannual 'William Tell' competition. A pair of 2nd TFTS
aircraft can be seen here getting airborne from Tyndall in October 1988.
Peter R. Foster

Right:
**Once again the swamps of
southern Georgia make a
magnificent setting for this
quartet of 128th TFS Eagles. The
aircraft depicted here,
75-0040/68/71 and the group
commander's aircraft, have all
seen operational service in other
theatres, primarily with the 36th
TFW at Bitburg in West
Germany.** *Don Spering/AIR*

Far right:
**F-15A 75-0040 was one of the
many aircraft to spend a period
in open storage at Robins AFB in
1980 when the severe spares
problem had recently caused the
1st TFW to fail its ORI. It was,
however, subsequently reissued
to the 33rd TFW at Eglin AFB
before being passed to the
Georgia ANG in 1986.**
Don Spering/AIR

The fine flying weather and clear blue skies revealed in this shot taken at
Tyndall AFB are deceptive, because the Gulf of Mexico can brew up a
hurricane at a moment's notice. However, the sea range area is one of
the few live firing areas for both heat-seeking and radar-guided missiles
available to the USAF and as such not only the 325th TTW, but all air
defence units, deploy here on a regular basis for live weapons practice.
Peter R. Foster

Above:
A sight long forgotten in Europe are such juicy targets as these flightlines. Here we have a line-up of 1st, 2nd and 97th TFTS aircraft at Tyndall AFB in October 1988. *Peter R. Foster*

Top:
Although the APG-63 radar is considered one of the most effective air defence radars today, Israel proved that the day of the dog fighter is not over and for this reason close combat weapons are essential. The AIM-9L/M Sidewinder heat-seeking missiles with an all-aspect parameter must therefore rank as probably the most lethal weapon available to the air defender today. The normal armament of the Eagle will include four such missiles which, in this docile state, belie that capability. *Peter R. Foster*

Left:

Left:
The July 1981 Tiger Meet hosted by the 53rd TFS at Bitburg was perhaps the last time that such lurid colour schemes would be allowed by USAFE. Subsequent events have seen just tiger-striped fin-tips and a tiger's head below the cockpit. Fortunately other air forces still enter into the spirit of things, but in 1991 when the event may well be staged at Bitburg again, things might have changed. *Peter R. Foster*

Right:
The latest unit to receive the F-15 has been the 101st FIS Massachusetts ANG which joined the 'Eagle Club' in 1988, taking on 23 F-15s from the 5th FIS at Minot which de-activated at the same time. The unit, in common with other air defence units, maintains an alert commitment – theirs being at Loring AFB, Maine, a role they acquired from the 49th FIS when they de-activated. *Regent Dansereau*

Far left:
F-15A 76-0026/LA, in the markings of the 'Triple Nickle' commander, breaks hard over the Arizona terrain. This aircraft, along with many assigned to the 58th TFTW (latterly 405TTW), have previously served with the 36th TFW at Bitburg although this particular aircraft came to the unit via the 33rd TFW at Eglin AFB. *Frank B. Mormillo*

Left:
The stillness of the ramp at Nellis revealed in this shot is strange, for once operations begin the feverish activity cannot be equalled by any other air base in the world. This pair of 58th TFS Eagles therefore wait with patience for the fun to begin. *Frank B. Mormillo*

Based at Eglin AFB, the 33rd TFW is the only unit to equip with the F-15C then the F-15A and then the F-15C again. This was primarily due the unit being charged with the work-up of the 18th TFW prior to the deployment to the Far East. Here F-15A 76-0045/EG, a former 36th TFW mount, taxis past one of the hangars at Tyndall AFB during the 1982 'William Tell' competition at which it fared less favourably than most of the other teams. Eglin was the first to adopt the blue band on the inside of the fin with an Eagle's head portrayed in the centre. Variations on this theme have subsequently been adopted by other units. *Peter R. Foster*

Having operated all variants of the Eagle with the exception of the 'C' model, the 40STTW is unique. Here F-15A 76-0067 of 555th TFTS, in company with F-15D 81-0063, take off from Luke's inner runway during October 1988. *Peter R. Foster*

Taken mid-way through Elgin's re-equipment programme for the second time, this picture shows F-15A 75-0078/EG on the tanker's port wing, whilst F-15D 82-0047/EG prepares to take its turn after the South Carolina F-16 drops back to formate on the starboard side.
Don Spering/AIR

Marked for the use of the 1st Air Force commander, F-15B 76-0126 sports the 'LY' tail code now associated with the 48th FIS at Langley AFB. Both remaining former ADC units have been allocated tail codes and the other, the 318th FIS at McChord, adopted the code 'TC', finally dragging the last vestige of the high vis ADC days into TAC commonality. *Peter R. Foster*

Above right:
One of the shortest-lived F-15 units has been the 5th FIS at Minot AFB. The unit received the jet to replace its ageing F-106 Delta Darts, only to come under a policy change some 12 months later which saw the unit de-activate completely. However, the aircraft were passed on to the Air National Guard for service with the 101st FIS at Otis ANGB. *Doug Remington*

Below right:
The 318th at McChord initially adopted their very fine blue marks that previously adorned the Delta Darts, but now they are having to fall in line with TAC policy and are replacing these with a 'TC' tail code. The unit was also scheduled to de-activate in late 1989, deviating from the original planned scheme of re-equipping with the F-16 Fighting Falcon. The F-15s will then be re-distributed into the Air National Guard. *Pat Martin*

Far right:
The major logistics centres at both Ogden and Warner-Robins AFBs operate a small fleet of type-related aircraft on various modification trials. At Warner-Robins, which is the prime ALC for the Eagle, F-15A 77-0068 has been on unit strength for most of its career having only served briefly with the 33rd TFW in 1978. This aircraft had, in 1980, received a 'WR' tail code obviously for Warner-Robins. However, due to a clash with the 81st TFW, this was soon changed to 'RG'. *Chris Pocock*

TAC's only frontline Wing to still operate the 'A' variant of the Eagle is the 49th TFW. In spite of its age the crews consistently achieve good results over their more up-to-date brothers. At the 1988 'William Tell' meet they took top place honours. Here F-15s 77-0086 and 77-0067 are seen climbing out of Tyndall AFB during the 1982 meet. *Peter R. Foster*

Following a period of work-up at Eglin AFB, the first US Wing to receive the 'C' model of the Eagle was the 18th TFW at Kadena. One of the prime assets of this variant was the ability to utilise the 'FAST' packs which, in Okinawa's isolated position, would in a time of hostility be a great asset. The Wing has retained the same aircraft for the last 10 years with the loss of only four jets. Here 78-0470/ZZ is seen over the Pacific during a pre-ORI exercise in November 1987. *Peter R. Foster*

Above a rippling carpet of cloud, 78-0470/ZZ slips away from the tanker on 'Mobile Eight' aerial refuelling track during November 1987, having taken on 2,000lb of fuel.
Peter R. Foster

One of the problems of operating from Kadena on Okinawa is the close proximity of the sea. In fact the runway begins almost on the seashore, at a position where the Marines came ashore in 1945. All aircraft from this island base are therefore subject to salt water corrosion, so each aircraft must taxi through the wash apron on a regular basis. Here 78-0494/ZZ of 44th TFS is seen being given the full treatment.
Toshiki Kudo

Left:
Silhouetted against the glistening Pacific, F-15C 78-0505/ZZ holds formation on KC-135Q 00336 of the 376th SW whilst acting as tanker support during the war games leading up to the unit's ORI in November 1987. *Peter R. Foster*

Below:
Kadena aircraft indicate their individual squadron allocation by the outer stripe of the triangle on the fin. In this case the yellow is for the 12th TFS, whilst the aircraft's serial has been suitably doctored to act as the squadron commander's mount. The 67th's colour is red, and the 44th's black. The triangle retains all three colours although in a different order. *Peter R. Foster*

Refuelling has to be accomplished even under tactical conditions which would result in the tanker flying a racetrack pattern. It is obvious from this picture that such refuelling can be accomplished during the turn. The aircraft concerned here is 78-0515/ZZ of 12th TFS 18th TFW.
Peter R. Foster

AFFTC at Edwards AFB undertakes many varied programmes connected with both flight trials and system updates. F-15D 79-0013/ED depicted here is involved in radar trials concerning the APG-70 radar and the legend on the fin reflects this. The photograph, however, was taken at Peterson AFB, Colorado, in April 1986 with the Rockies resplendent in the background. *Don Jay*

Europe is perhaps considered as the USAF's frontline and as such the equipment deployed to the theatre has to be at the top of the range. Subsequently, the units assigned to USAFE have seen continual equipment updates over the years. The 32nd TFS at Soesterberg initially received the F-15A model with 'Coronet Sandpiper'; however, when the 'C' model was available it was the first to transition. Pictured here on 'Carrol ART' during their 'William Tell' work-up are 79-0027/18. *Peter R. Foster*

Top:
The latest major command to receive the Eagle has been Alaska. Initially, only the 43rd TFS received the type, but then the 54 TFS was activated on the 'C' model, quickly followed by the transition of the 43rd to the same variant. Seen here, as displayed on most of the Wing's aircraft, is a map of Alaska with 'Anchorage' emblazoned across it. *Peter R. Foster*

Above:
Most Eagles these days adopt some kind of motif on the inside of the vertical stabilisers. Alaskan ones have the seven stars representing the plough, together with the pole star. This aircraft, 79-0075/AK, was formerly on the strength of Bitburg, whilst the centreline tank has a small map of Alaska stencilled upon it. *Peter R. Foster*

Far left:
As well as its excess of power, the big wing of the Eagle makes it a very manoeuvrable aircraft. Being put through its paces in a dirty condition is 80-0003/BT of 22nd TFS. *Peter R. Foster*

Left:
Two ends of the spectrum are graphically portrayed at the 1984 Alconbury display as F-15C 80-0003/BT taxis in whilst the replica Eindecker makes a 'high-speed' flypast. *Peter R. Foster*

Below:
With the 'wolf's' head on the inside of the port fin and an 'IS' tail code, this aircraft is easily identifiable as belonging to the 57th FIS at Keflavik in Iceland. In Phantom days the sound of a 'Slogin' callsign brought enthusiasts from far and wide, but since the arrival of the Eagle the unit has been more prolific within the central region. This shot of 80-0042 was taken at RAF Alconbury during one of the unit's DACT detachments. *Peter R. Foster*

Left:
Pictured whilst on a visit to Soesterberg in the Netherlands, 80-0006 of 22nd TFS resides in a typical European shelter complex. The necessity of such shelters – or TAB-Vs as they are called by the Americans – is well recognised in ensuring that SACEUR's limited assets are made as survivable as possible. *Herman J. Sixma*

With storm clouds gathering, this 81 fiscal F-15C from the 32nd TFS lands at Alconbury bathed in the light from the setting sun following a DACT sortie against the 527th AS F-5Es. This jet, along with five others, was delivered to Soesterberg a year or so later than the original deliveries to increase the unit's effective strength. *Peter R. Foster*

Sporting Luke's unique type of serial presentation, the peeling TAC badge and 'LA' tailcode belie the fact that 80-0107 is in fact the first Saudi F-15D. Akin to all other users of the type, initial crew training has been undertaken under the watchful eye of the 58th TFTW and latterly the 405th TTW. Japan detached its first four F-15DJs to Luke at the same period as Saudi Arabia; Israel on the other hand used USAF aircraft although the photograph on page 5 shows one of the IDF F-15As at Luke. *Peter R. Foster*

Far left:
Prior to the introduction of the 'Strike Eagle', several tactical colour schemes were tested out utilising the services of the 422nd TES at Nellis AFB. Although not the chosen scheme, this one displayed by 82-0028/WA was arguably the most attractive, and is seen here at Peterson AFB in April 1987.
Don Jay

Left:
Arrival on the ramp at a visiting base does not necessarily signify the end of the sortie. Apart from shutting the systems down, this pilot then begins the period of aircraft turn-around.
Peter R. Foster

SSGT EUGENE HOLLEY
SRA DERF WILKERSON
AMN DALE HOOVEN

RESCUE
EMERGENCY ENTRANCE
CONTROL ON OTHER
SIDE

2038

Left:
The F-15 is a big jet and the distance to the ground from the cockpit is one to be treated with respect. Here a pilot from the 1st TFW prepares to leave his mount whilst visiting Tyndall AFB in October 1988.
Peter R. Foster

Right:
Loaded with three external tanks, 83-0015/FF begins its taxi run at RAF Alconbury following a weekend visit to the UK whilst detached to Bremgarten during 'Coronet Mohawk' in August 1986. As will be seen, the practice of inscribing the aircraft with the squadron number, in this case 94th TFS, had begun in earnest. *Peter R. Foster*

Far left:

In this view taken during the 1988 'William Tell' meet at Tyndall AFB, all of the 1st TFW aircraft were inscribed with the Wing details whilst the individual aircraft serials were displayed underneath. The unit stood a very good chance of winning the trophy for the best turned-out aircraft, and the shine on the titanium box around the reheat area gives a mirror finish. *Peter R. Foster*

Left:

Although many units have opted for outline badges in an attempt to create a complete illusion of low visibility, if your adversary gets close enough to see actual unit badges then you are no doubt already dead! However, the 33rd TFW has always retained full-colour badges which, for the sake of the team representing the Wing at the 1980 'William Tell' meet, was applied to each aircraft. *Peter R. Foster*

Right:
For the 1988 'William Tell' meet the 33rd had only applied the Wing badge which can be seen behind this crew chief who is attaching the AIM-9M seeker head cover to the missile.
Peter R. Foster

Far right:
Eglin has at last settled down to receive the final batches of the air defence Eagle. Seen here at a Homestead AFB 'open-house' in 1988 is F-15C 86-0147/EG, which has allowed the earlier 84 fiscal aircraft to begin transitioning to the 36th TFW in Europe.
Peter R. Foster

Right:
The first unit to receive the Strike Eagle was the 461st TFTS at Luke AFB commanded by Lt-Col Trotter. The unit's first two aircraft – 86-0187/LA marked as '461 TFTS', and 86-0186/LA as '405 TTW' – are seen here over Luke AFB in October 1988. *Peter R. Foster*

Far right:
As with such types as the F-104 Starfighter, the dual-seat variety of the F-15 has been built in the United States. This particular jet operated with the unit at Luke as 79-0283 before being delivered to Japan where it was re-serialled 12-8052. It is seen here at Komaki AB in the markings of 202 Hikotai during November 1987. *Peter R. Foster*

APPENDIX

F-15 Units

Royal Saudi Air Force

Unit	Variant	Markings	Base
5 Sqn	F-15C/D		At Taif
6 Sqn	F-15C/D		Khamis Mushayt
13 Sqn	F-15C/D		Dhahran

Israeli AF/DF

106 Fighter Sqn	F-15C/D		Tel Nov
133 Fighter Sqn	F-15A/B		Tel Nov

Japanese Air Self Defence Force

Air Proving Wing	F-15J/DJ	APW in an arrow	Gifu
201 Hikotai	F-15J/DJ		Chitose
202 Hikotai	F-15J/DJ	Gold clay image of a warrior	Nyutabaru
203 Hikotai	F-15J/DJ	Geometrically-shaped teddy bear	Chitose
204 Hikotai	F-15J/DJ	An eagle's head	Hyakuri
303 Hikotai	F-15J/DJ	Stylised green dragon	Komatsu
304 Hikotai*	F-15J/DJ	Long-nosed goblin	Tsuiki

(*Due to convert from F-4EJ to F-15J during 1989.)

United States Air Force

Unit	Variant	Markings	Base
TACTICAL AIR COMMAND — DIRECT REPORTING UNITS			
Tactical Air Warfare Center			
4485 TS 3246 TW	F-15A/C	Black/white check 'OT'	Eglin AFB, Fla
3246 TW	F-15A-E	White band/red diamonds 'ET'*	Eglin AFB, Fla

(*Unit recoded from 'AD' during 1989.)

Tactical Fighter Weapons Center			
422 TES 57 FWW	F-15C/D	Black/yellow check 'WA'	Nellis AFB, Nev
433 TES 57 FWW	F-15A/B	Black/yellow check 'WA'	Nellis AFB, Nev

(*The F-15 FWS/TFWC use aircraft on a pool basis whilst the 433 TES has since de-activated on the type.)

Air Force Flight Test Center			
6512 TS	F-15A-E	Blue fin stripe 'ED'	Edwards AFB, Ca

AIR DEFENCE TACTICAL AIR COMMAND

1st Air Force

23rd Air Division

48 FIS	F-15A/B	Blue, 4 white stars 'LY'	Langley AFB, Va

25th Air Division

5 FIS	F-15A/B	5 Yellow stars	Minot AFB, ND

(*De-activated during 1987 and aircraft passed to 101FIS Massachusetts ANG at Otis ANGB.)

318 FIS	F-15A/B	Blue fin tip 'TC'	McChord AFB, WA

(*De-activated in late 1989 and aircraft transferred to 123 FIS Oregon ANG.)

Air Defense Weapons Centre

1 TFTS 325 TTW	F-15A/B	Red fin tip 'TY'	Tyndall AFB, Fla
2 TFTS 325 TTW	F-15A/B	Yellow fin tip 'TY'	Tyndall AFB, Fla
97 TFTS 325 TTW	F-15A/B	Blue fin tip 'TY'	Tyndall AFB, Fla

Air Forces Iceland

57 FIS	F-15C/D	Black/white check 'IS'	Keflavik AB, Iceland

(*Some aircraft wear a wolf's head on the inside of the port fin, whilst others have a map of Iceland on the inside of the port fin.)

Far left:
Built as 81-0068, this F-15DJ is now serialled 32-8057 and in the service of 202 Hikotai by whom it is put through its paces at the 1987 Tsuiki air show.
Peter R. Foster

9th Air Force

27 TFS 1 TFW	F-15C/D	Yellow fin tip 'FF'		Langley AFB, Va
71 TFS 1 TFW	F-15C/D	Red fin tip 'FF'		Langley AFB, Va
94 TFS 1 TFW	F-15C/D	Blue fin tip 'FF'		Langley AFB, Va
334 TFS 4 TFW	F-15E	Blue fin tip 'SJ'		Seymour Johnson AFB
335 TFS 4 TFW	F-15E	Green fin tip 'SJ'		Seymour Johnson AFB
336 TFS 4 TFW	F-15E	Yellow fin tip 'SJ'		Seymour Johnson AFB

(*Wing due to re-equip with the Strike Eagle during 1989/90.)

58 TFS 33 TFW	F-15C/D	Blue fin tip 'EG'	Eglin AFB, Fla
59 TFS 33 TFW	F-15C/D	Yellow fin tip 'EG'	Eglin AFB, Fla
60 TFS 33 TFW	F-15C/D	Red fin tip 'EG'	Eglin AFB, Fla

(*All 33rd TFW aircraft wear a broad blue band with an eagle's head on the inside of the fins.)

832nd Air Division

426 TFTS 405 TTW	F-15A/B/D	Red fin tip 'LA'	Luke AFB, Az
461 TFTS 405 TTW	F-15E	Yellow fin tip 'LA'	Luke AFB, Az
550 TFTS 405 TTW	F-15E	Black/silver wings 'LA'	Luke AFB, Az
555 TFTS 405 TTW	F-15A/B/D	Green/5 white stars 'LA'	Luke AFB, Az

(*The unit was originally assigned to the 58th TFTW at Luke AFB but the size of the unit became too unwealdy and therefore the 405th TTW was activated to handle Eagle operations. This left the 58th with the F-4C Phantom and F-104G Starfighter to administer, but has now transitioned to the F-16 Fighting Falcon.)

833rd Air Division

7 TFS 49 TFW	F-15A/B	Blue/white check 'HO'	Holloman AFB, NM
8 TFS 49 TFW	F-15A/B	Yellow fin tip 'HO'	Holloman AFB, NM
9 TFS 49 TFW	F-15A/B	Red fin tip 'HO'	Holloman AFB, NM

Air National Guard

101 FIS 102 FIG	F-15A/B	'Massachusetts'	Otis ANGB, Mas
122 TFS 159 TFW	F-15A/B	'Louisiana' in a red, blue, green or yellow fin tip	New Orleans NAS
123 FIS 142 FIG	F-15A/B	'Oregon' on a deep crimson scroll at base of fin	Portland IAP Oregon
128 TFS 116 TFW	F-15A/B	'Georgia' outlined in yellow on a black band edged in red	Dobbins AFB, Ga
199 FIS 154 FIG	F-15A/B	'Hawaii' on a red and yellow band	Hickham AFB, Hawaii

Alaskan Air Command

43 TFS 21 TFW	F-15C/D	Blue fin tip 'AK'	Elmendorf AFB, Alaska
54 TFS 21 TFW	F-15C/D	Yellow fin tip 'AK'	Elmendorf AFB, Alaska

(*All 21 TFW aircraft wear a deep blue band with stars representing the Plough on the inside of the fins.)

Pacific Air Force

12 TFS 18 TFW	F-15C/D	Yellow triangle 'ZZ'	Kadena AFB, Okinawa
44 TFS 18 TFW	F-15C/D	Black triangle 'ZZ'	Kadena AFB, Okinawa
67 TFS 18 TFW	F-15C/D	Red triangle 'ZZ'	Kadena AFB, Okinawa

(*All 18 TFW aircraft wear a Shogun figure on inside of fins.)

US AIR FORCES EUROPE

17th Air Force

32 TFS 78 TFG	F-15C/D	Orange band outlined in green 'CR'	Soesterberg AB, NL
22 TFS 36 TFW	F-15C/D	Red fin tip 'BT'	Bitburg AFB, WG
53 TFS 36 TFW	F-15C/D	Yellow or tiger striped fin tip 'BT'	Bitburg AFB, WG
525 TFS 36 TFW	F-15C/D	Blue fin tip 'BT'	Bitburg AFB, WG

F-15 losses

Date	Serial/Code	Unit	Notes
14.10.75	73-0088 LA	58 TFTW	Crashed at Luke AFB, Az
28.02.77	74-0129 WA	57 FWW	Crashed on range following collision with F-5E
06.12.77	75-0085 WA	57 FWW	Crashed on Nellis Ranges
08.02.78	73-0097 LA	58 TFTW	Written off in ground accident
17.04.78	75-0059 BT	36 TFW	Crashed into North Sea off Cromer
15.06.78	76-0047 BT	36 TFW	Crashed into North Sea during ACT
06.07.78	76-0053 BT	36 TFW	Crashed nr Daun, W Germany
01.09.78	75-0018 FF	1 FTW	Crashed in Atlantic off Virginia
19.12.78	75-0063 BT	36 TFW	Crashed nr Aalhorn, W Germany
28.12.78	75-0064 BT	36 TFW	Crashed nr Daun, W Germany
29.12.78	74-0136 WA	57 FWW	Crashed at Nellis AFB
16.02.79	77-0107 HO	49 TFW	Crashed at Nellis Ranges
12.03.79	77-0076 HO	49 TFW	
25.04.79	77-0167	MACAIR	Crashed nr Fredericktown on test flight
03.06.79	76-0035 BT	36 TFW	Crashed on landing at Bitburg
13.09.79	76-0085 WA	57 FWW	
03.10.79	77-0072 HO	49 TFW	Crashed after colliding with 77-0061/HO
04.03.80	75-0070 BT	36 TFW	Crashed nr Baden-Baden, W Germany
06.03.80	76-0082 BT	36 TFW	Crashed nr Bitburg, W Germany
10.03.80	76-0023 FF	1 TFW	Burnt out on flight line at Langley AFB
25.07.80	76-0013 BT	36 TFW	
21.01.81	77-0164 WA	57 FWW	Crashed following a collision with F-5E 74-1517 over Nellis Ranges
17.02.81	76-0065 LA	405 TTW	Crashed into Pacific

Date	Serial	Unit	Notes
23.06.81	79-0040 BT	36 TFW	Crashed 15 miles from Bremen, W Germany
12.09.81	80-0007 BT	36 TFW	Crashed on landing at Soesterberg
02.11.81	75-0051 EG	33 TFW	Crashed nr Panama City after collision with another F-15 on refuelling mission
15.12.81	73-0106 LA	405 TTW	Crashed nr Phoenix, Az
06.04.82	78-0524 ZZ	18 TFW	Crashed into Pacific 40 miles NW of Okinawa
22.12.82	80-0025 BT	36 TFW	Crashed nr Herschbach, W Germany
28.12.82	78-0481 ZZ	18 TFW	Collided with 78-0540/ZZ 92 miles NE of Okinawa crashing into Pacific
28.12.82	78-0540 ZZ	18 FTW	as above
04.01.83	80-0036 FF	1 TFW	
04.02.83	76-0081 BT	36 TFW	
09.05.83	77-0094 HO	49 TFW	Crashed at White Sands range, N Mexico
01.06.83	79-0071 BT	36 TFW	Crashed nr Kusel following collision with 80-0008/BT
01.06.83	80-0008 BT	36 TFW	as above
06.10.83	75-0076 EG	33 TFW	Crashed 45 miles N of Cold Lake after colliding with F-5E 74-1509
20.10.83	12-8053	202 Hikotai	Crashed into Pacific 110 miles E of Nyutabaru
10.04.84	79-0044 BT	36 TFW	Crashed nr Lommersdorf, W Germany
17.08.84	75-0087 TY	325 FWW	Crashed into Gulf of Mexico after colliding with F-4E 68-0535/RS
24.06.85	74-0087 AK	21 TFW	Crashed into Yukon River, Alaska
31.08.85	81-0039 FF	1 TFW	
09.09.85	74-0094 AK	21 TFW	Crashed in Alaska
05.11.85	74-0090 AK	21 TFW	
16.12.85			Crashed into Gulf of Mexico
02.01.86	80-0037 IS	57 FIS	Crashed into Atlantic
07.01.86	79-0061 BT	36 TFW	Crashed nr Rimschweiler after colliding with 80-0032/BT nr Zweibrücken
07.01.86	80-0032 BT	36 TFW	as above
15.01.86	76-0023	5 FIS	Crashed in Guadalupe Mountains
00.09.86	610	6 SDN/RSAF	Collided with 611 nr Khamis and although landed both thought to be w/o
00.09.86	611	6 SDN/RSAF	as above
09.03.87	HO	49 TFW	Crashed 3 miles SE of Holloman AFB
13.03.87	42-8840	204 Hikotai	Crashed into sea 100 miles E of Hyakuri
10.04.87		/IDF	an F-15D
19.05.87	78-0495 ZZ	18 TFW	Crashed into Pacific
08.06.87	81-0056 FF	1 TFW	Crashed in Virginia (also quoted as 06.08.87)
03.09.87	77-0075 HO	49 TFW	Could this be 09.03.87?
01.10.87		48 FIS	Crashed in Apalachicola Forest
24.11.87	75-0056	128 TFS	Collided with F-16B 79-0419 466 TFS near Wadley, Ga
29.06.88	22-8804	303 Hikotai	Collided with wingman, crashing into Sea of Japan
29.06.88	22-8808	303 Hikotai	as above
16.08.88		/IDF	Collided with wingman crashing near Dead Sea
16.08.88		/IDF	as above
30.08.88	511	13 SDN/RSAF	Crashed nr Al Hesa, Saudi Arabia
08.11.88	80-0017 AK	21 TFW	Crashed 5 miles NW of Kodiak, Alaska
01.05.89	76-0138 TY	325 TTW	Crashed into Gulf of Mexico 65nm SE of Tyndall AFB
08.07.89	? EG	33TFW	Crashed in Alabama
10.08.89	? HO	49TFW	Crashed 60 miles north of Holloman AFB
28.12.89	? EG	33TFW	Crashed into Gulf of Mexico 40 miles SE of Apalachicola, Fla
11.01.90	? AK	21TFW	Crashed into Big Mount Susitana approx 30 miles SW of Anchorage, Alaska

F-15 Serials

Serial	Variant	Operator
71-0280 – 0289	F-15A	USAF
71-0290 – 0291	TF-15A	USAF later redesignated F-15B
72-0113 – 0120	F-15A	USAF 20116/17/18/20 later to Israel
73-0085 – 0107	F-15A	USAF
73-0108 – 0114	TF-15A	USAF later redesignated F-15B
74-0081 – 0136	F-15A	USAF
74-0137 – 0142	TF-15A	USAF later redesignated F-15B
74-0143 – 0157	F-15	USAF canx
75-0018 – 0081	F-15A	USAF
75-0082 – 0089	TF-15A	USAF later redesignated F-15B
75-0090 – 0124	F-15	USAF canx
76-0008 – 0120	F-15A	USAF
76-0121 – 0123	F-15	USAF canx
76-0124 – 0142	TF-15A	USAF later redesignated F-15B
76-1505 – 1523	F-15A	FMS/Israel
76-1524 – 1525	TF-15A	FMS/Israel
77-0061 – 0153	F-15A	USAF
77-0154 – 0168	TF-15A	USAF later redesignated F-15B
78-0468 – 0550	F-15C	USAF
78-0551 – 0560	F-15C	USAF canx
78-0561 – 0574	F-15D	USAF

64

Far right:
The serialling system reflects the fiscal year of introduction into service, the type of aircraft and role as well as individual identification. F-15DJ 32-8060 is pictured preparing to taxi.
Peter R. Foster

Serial	Type	Operator
79-0004 – 0014	F-15D	USAF
79-0015 – 0081	F-15C	USAF
79-0280 – 0281	F-15J	FMS/Japan 02-8801-8802
79-0282 – 0285	F-15DJ	FMS/Japan 12-8051-8054
80-0002 – 0053	F-15C	USAF
80-0054 – 0061	F-15D	USAF
80-0062 – 0106	F-15C	FMS/Saudi Arabia
80-0107 – 0110	F-15D	FMS/Saudi Arabia
81-0002 – 0003	F-15C	FMS/Saudi Arabia
81-0020 – 0056	F-15C	USAF
81-0057 – 0060	F-15C	USAF canx
81-0061 – 0065	F-15D	USAF
81-0066 – 0067	F-15D	USAF canx
81-0068 – 0071	F-15C	FMS/? could these be F-15DJs 32-8057-060?
82-0008 – 0043	F-15C	USAF
82-0044 – 0049	F-15D	USAF
83-0010 – 0043	F-15C	USAF
83-0046 – 0050	F-15D	USAF
83-0052 – 0053	F-15DJ	FMS/Japan 52-8061-8062?
83-0054 – 0062	F-15C	FMS/Isreal
83-0063 – 0064	F-15D	FMS/Israel
84-0001 – 0031	F-15C	USAF
84-0042 – 0046	F-15D	USAF
85-0093 – 0128	F-15C	USAF
85-0129 – 0134	F-15D	USAF
86-0143 – 0180	F-15C	USAF
86-0181 – 0182	F-15D	USAF
86-0183 – 0190	F-15E	USAF
87-0169 – 0210	F-15E	USAF
88-1667 – 1708	F-15E	USAF
88-	F-15	FMS/Saudia Arabia (12 A/C)
88-	F-15	FMS/Israel (5 A/C)
89-	F-15E	USAF (42 a/c)
90-	F-15E	USAF (42 a/c)
91-	F-15E	USAF (24 a/c)

F-16 FIGHTING FALCON

PETER R. FOSTER

WP
AF
81 675

LONDON

IAN ALLAN LTD

PREFACE

Previous page:
PACAF saw introduction of the F–16 at an early stage, with the 8th TFW at Kunsan in South Korea receiving early Block 10 aircraft. These were soon replaced with Block 15 aircraft incorporating many of the service modifications. As a unit the 8th has become a prime test one for Fighting Falcon operations as South Korea is considered one of the most realistic peace-time scenarios available to USAF aircrew. As an aircraft the F–16 has proved itself rugged and reliable, lending weight to its overseas sales potential. The photograph depicts 81- 0675/WP of the 80th TFS just prior to lift-off.
Greg Meggs

There are now some 15 operators of the General Dynamics F–16, an aircraft which, in a similar fashion to its predecessor as the low cost lightweight fighter, the F–104 Starfighter, started from humble beginnings and faced a tremendous uphill struggle to find acceptance. However unlike Kelly Johnson's 'missile with a man in it', the F–16 has gone from strength to strength; and although it costs in the region of $17 million, a copy is still considered relatively cheap by current standards.

This portfolio was conceived to portray the Fighting Falcon in operational service, but it soon became apparent that with 16 Wings alone within the United States Air Force, it would be impossible to do justice to all the users within a book of this size. Therefore I have decided to attack the problem by introducing to the connoisseurs of aviation a selection of some of the best contemporary photographs of this remarkable aeroplane presently available. Virtually all of these are in active service with units of the air forces of the United States and its NATO partners. Perhaps a follow-up at some point can do justice to some of the lesser-known users. To this end I hope the reader will find as much enjoyment in reading this publication as I have had in compiling it.

Peter Foster
Brampton

FIGHTING FALCON

By January 1988 somewhere in the region of 2,000 General Dynamics F–16 'Fighting Falcons' had been produced off four production lines in the United States and Europe. Its users span the world with examples on all three major continents – and two operators have gone on to prove it in combat.

Probably the most widely used fly-by-wire combat system anywhere in the world, the F–16's acceptance from the embryo stage was nevertheless nearly a traumatic experience. In the late 1960s and very early 1970s, when the dollar was far from its previous healthy position, those responsible for ensuring that the best value was obtained from an admittedly large defence budget greeted the proposal for a low cost lightweight fighter (LWF) with some considerable interest. However in opposition to such a proposal sat the US Air Force, which ultimately would have to operate any new type. It somewhat naturally was concerned that any new acquisition would seriously affect the number of McDonnell-Douglas F–15 Eagles that could be purchased, thus compromising any benefits to be gained by a low-cost lightweight fighter.

In spite of all the initial misgivings shown by the military, the F–16 as we know it was given a boost in 1974 when Secretary of Defence James Schlesinger revealed that Department of Defence proposals for the LWF envisaged the possible acquisition of a derivative of greatly enhanced capability, this being known as the ACF (Air Combat Fighter),

a type radically different from the unsophisticated and inexpensive day superiority fighter of the initial proposals. This, coupled with Schlesinger's decision to provide an additional five Tactical Fighter Wings, meant that the new fighter could be procured as well as the highly sophisticated all-weather F–15 Eagle, and disposed of virtually all resistance overnight. From then on General Dynamics' project gained momentum, the company discovering more influential supporters than it ever knew existed.

The F–16 – or rather the two YF–16 prototypes – emerged at the end of the LWF evaluation programme in January 1975 as the successful candidate. (The more sophisticated YF–17 went on to greater things as the F–18 Hornet, but that is another story.) Following the evaluation trials the prototypes were joined by a batch of 15 development aircraft, four F–16B two-seaters and 11 F–16As. At this time it was becoming clear that the F–16 was to become one of the more significant combat aircraft of the 1970s and 1980s, especially with the announcement on 11 September 1974 that the winner of the LWF competition would be ordered in quantity for the USAF.

Into Service

The first production F–16 was formally accepted by the USAF on 17 August 1978 and the first delivery to an operational unit occurred on 6 January 1979. Tasked with the introduction

of the Fighting Falcon into service was the 388th TFW, which had gained much glory with the venerable F–105 Thunderchief in South-East Asia and had then re-activated at the unit's home base of Hill AFB, Ogden, Utah, on the F–4D Phantom. Ogden was also chosen to become the Air Logistics Centre (ALC) for the F–16, and thus the 388th had been a logical choice to bring the aircraft into service.

The 388th's 4th Tactical Fighter Squadron was the first squadron to achieve initial operational status with the F–16, on 12 November 1980, and in March of the following year the unit took 12 aircraft as 'Coronet Falcons' to Flesland in Norway for the first of many overseas deployments. The 388th was also instrumental in adding further proof to the aircraft's capability by winning the Royal Air Force-sponsored tactical bombing competition at Lossiemouth in June 1981, defeating the RAF's Jaguar and Buccaneers as well as the USAFE's F–111Es.

Running concurrently with the 388th's re-equipment was that of the 8th TFW at Kunsan, South Korea, which began converting to Block 10 aircraft in September 1981, the first two aircraft (90397/98) having been at Hill prior to delivery in May. This was followed shortly afterwards by the 50th TFW at Hahn in West Germany which received five F–16s for maintenance training from McDill on 10 September. Prior to this the Belgian Air Force was providing four aircraft per week on cross-servicing sorties. The first European squadron to equip with the F–16 was the 313th TFS, although it was originally reported that the 496th TFS would have the honour, and it began work-up at Zaragosa in Spain, returning to Hahn as an operational unit in the spring of 1982. The aircraft assigned to Hahn were from Block 15 and these had the larger horizontal tail surfaces and inlet hardpoints for AMRAAM missiles and LANTIRN sensors. The 8th at Kunsan also traded its Block 10 aircraft for Block 15, the original airframes returning re-assigned to the 363rd TFW at Shaw AFB, South Carolina, in 1982.

The 363rd had been redesignated a TFW on 1 October 1981 and received its first F–16A, 00528, by March 1982. The Wing's first squadron, the 17th TFS, was activated on 1 July 1982, followed by the 19th TFS on 1 April 1982. The 56th TFW at McDill was also redesignated a TTW on 1 October 1981, whilst the 31st TFW had preceded both on 30 March 1981 but was still at that time completely F–4D equipped.

Also in 1982 came the highly publicised conversion to the F–16 by the USAF's Thunderbirds display team, becoming the fourth squadron to be assigned to Nellis's 474th TFW which transitioned to the F–16 after the 56th TTW at McDill. The Thunderbirds had received their full quota of nine aircraft by September.

The first Air National Guard unit to receive the Fighting Falcon was the 157th TFS at McEntire ANGB, South California, which received 24 Block 10 aircraft mainly drawn from the Hill and McDill units. The unit completed its conversion to operational readiness by mid-1983.

AFRES was also due to receive the F–16 with the 466th TFS at Hill AFB trading in the last fighter 'Thuds' during 1983. At that time the programme for 'Reserve' and 'Guard' units to receive the F–16 included the 101st FIS at Otis ANGB, the 119th FIS at Atlantic City, the 123rd FIS at Portland and the 186th FIS at Great Falls.

In Europe, hot on the heels of the 50th TFW, came the re-equipment of the 401st TFW at Torrejon, Spain, a unit that was in the centre of delicate negotiations regarding the American presence in 1987. Initially Torrejon received Block 15 aircraft, but as happened with most units began to up-grade, re-assigning the early aircraft to Stateside units.

The continued up-grade of the aircraft avionics led to the introduction of the F–16C from Fiscal Year (FY) 83 onwards. The first unit to receive the type was the 312th TFTS at Luke AFB which formed in October 1984, whilst the 363rd TFW also began the transition to the type in November 1985, with the 33rd TFS leading the way. The Wing's 'A' models were then passed onto the 31st TTW at Homestead which at that time was still utilising the 'ZF' tail code although as far as the Fighting Falcon was concerned this was shortlived because the Wing changed to a more sensible 'HS' code on 1 December 1986. One squadron's worth of later-model FISCAL–83 F–16As were transferred to the newly-formed 432nd TFW at Misawa AB in northern Japan, although this unit too began receiving General Electric F110-engined F–16Cs with its re-equipment concurrent with the 86th TFW.

In Europe both the 50th TFW at Hahn and the 86th TFW at Ramstein were scheduled to receive the F–16C/D models and both units began transition in parallel, with the 86th receiving its first four aircraft direct from Fort Worth on 20 September 1985. These were F-16Cs 84-1238/39/40 and F-

Left
The 58th Tactical Training Wing at Luke AFB reverted to a Tactical Fighter Wing which operates two squadrons of F–16A/B aircraft and two of F–16C/D. It reports to the 832nd Air Division and, as is now a common practice, reflects this on F–16A 78-0018. This aircraft is the eighteenth production F–16A and originally saw service with the 388th TFW at Hill AFB. It is seen here at Luke AFB in May 1986. *Don Jay*

16D 84-1323. Hahn received its first C model aircraft by mid-December and this time it was the 496th TFS which began conversion first. These aircraft were all Pratt & Whitney F100-engined airframes and were destined to be the last USAF examples so equipped. From October 1986 all USAF aircraft were delivered with the General Electric F110 engine. The 86th TFW was therefore tasked with the service introduction of so engined F–16s and as a result began transferring its P & W F100-engined aircraft to the 50th TFW at Hahn.

The final unit to change to F-16 operations in Europe was the 52nd TFW at Spangdahlen which received its first F–16C on 26 March 1987. The Wing, unlike all other F–16 operators, intended to use the Fighting Falcon alongside the F–4G 'Wild Weasel' Phantoms in joint squadrons – a formation jocularly known as the 'Odd Couple'.

At home the USAF's longed-for goal of achieving 40 tactical Wings by the mid-1990s had faded to 37 because of continued budget restraints. The DoD therefore now concentrates on up-grading existing units, with Fiscal Year requests in 1988 and 1989 totalling 360 aircraft.

This up-grading continued with the 159th FIS Florida ANG receiving its first four aircraft in August 1986 along with the 182nd TFS Texas ANG at Kelly AFB, both of which were recipients of former 50th TFW F–16As. The 134th TFS Vermont ANG at Burlington also began transition from the F–4D to F–16 in mid-1986, its aircraft being predominantly former 388th TFW machines, from the de-actuated 16th TFS.

For the future, the 8th TFW at Kunsan began transition onto the F–16C in October 1987, with its 'A' models returning to the States for use by the 347th TFW at Moody AFB, whilst the 184th TFG at McConnell started to re-equip with the F–16A during the same period, the 161st TFTS activating for the purpose on 12 September 1987.

Other units scheduled to receive the F–16 included 160th TRS Alabama ANG and 184th TFS Arkansas ANG in spring 1988, and 465th TFS (the second AFRES unit) at Tinker AFB, Oklahoma. The first air defence dedicated F–16As will go to the 114th TFTS Oregon ANG at Kingsley Field in early 1989 to be followed by the 194th FIS California ANG at Fresno in late 1989.

For the first time since converting the F–86 and F–80 for carrier use, the US Navy adopted a land-based fighter when it accepted the first of 26 F–16N Fighting Falcons to replace the ageing A–4 and F–5 aircraft of the Fighter Weapons 'Top Gun' school. The first aircraft was delivered on 30 April 1987 with all 22 single-seat and four two-seat aircraft due by the end of April 1988. The F–16N is basically a C model without the M61A1 20mm cannon, and is fitted with the F–16A APG66 radar.

'Sale of the Century'

There can be little doubt that having the USAF fully committed to the ACF concept and in particular the F–16 was an initial step by both Congress and GD to the more lucrative markets of Europe and the free world. The late 1970s was seen as the time of a ripe market with many of NATO's front-line second-generation jets nearing the end of their effectiveness. GD, along with Dassault-Breguet, Saab and Northrop, was eagerly canvassing the respective defence ministries of Holland, Denmark, Norway and Belgium in the hope of securing an initial order for approximately 350 aeroplanes.

To ease the selection process the four nations formed a body known as the Multi-national Fighter Programme Group (MFPG) early in 1974. Following the evaluation of the final four contenders – F–16, F–18, Mirage F–1 and Saab Euro-fighter (a Viggen derivative) – the F–16 emerged as the front-runner. The announcement of its victory was made at the 1975 Paris Air Show.

The initial order called for 348 aircraft, made up of 290 F–16As plus 58 two-seat F–16Bs. Holland, Belgium and Denmark have increased their quantities to allow for the replacement not only of the F–104 Starfighter as originally intended but also the Northrop/Canadair F–5 and Dassault Mirage V fleets.

Delivery of the first European production aircraft was off the SABCA line at Gossellies in the shape of F–16B FB01 on 23 March 1979, and it and the subsequent aircraft to roll off the Belgian line formed into a conversion unit at Beauvechain under the auspices of No 1 Wing. On 16 January 1981 the first squadron, No 349, Belgian AF, was officially assigned to NATO, being declared operational on 6 May. This was followed by No 350 Squadron (also at Beauvechain) in the interceptor role and subsequently Nos 23 and 31 Squadrons of No 10 Wing at Kleine Brogel. Belgium's original intention was for three wings of F–16s, the final wing to be No 2 at Florennes which will consist of Nos 1 and 2 Squadrons. The

Right
With one of the great Salt Lakes in the background, F–16A 78-0027/HI of the 466th TFS begins its approach over Ogden to Hill AFB. The unit has been joined by a second AFRES unit, the 302nd TFS at Luke AFB, which, consistent with US policy of upgrading its non-regular forces, began receiving factory-fresh 86 fiscal F–16Cs in the middle of 1987. The 302nd converted from the CH-3E which it had employed in the special operations role, and it now falls under the control of the 944th TFG, both units having activated on 1 July 1987. *Ted W. Van Geffen/ IAAP*

crews are currently undergoing conversion at Beauvechain.

The second nation to receive the F–16 in Europe was Holland when F–16B J259 was rolled out at Fokker's Schipole production line on 3 May 1979, followed shortly by the first F–16A, J212, both being delivered on 6 June of that year. However, rather than operate twinned squadrons the *Koninklijke Luchtmacht* chose to shut down each of the units converting to the F–16 for the year or so that the transition required. Initially the *Transitie en Conversie Afdeling* (TCA) at Leeuwarden was set up to handle F–16 conversion with the instructors at the beginning having undergone training at Hill AFB with the 388th TFW. No 322 Squadron, chosen to be the first to convert to the type, began transition at Leeuwarden in October 1979 with the unit completing conversion by the end of April 1981. No 322 was followed by No 323, also at Leeuwarden, before a second OCU was set up at Volkel to handle the transition by Nos 306, 311 and 312 Squadrons.

The TCA at Leeuwarden stayed in situ until 1 March 1986, handling the conversion for the air defence committed units, whilst the OCU at Volkel was hidden within the structure of No 311 Squadron. This has now passed on to No 315 Squadron at Twenthe which as the sixth squadron to convert will now handle the transition of the three remaining squadrons, Nos 313, 314 and 316, as well as new pilots for the existing squadrons.

Denmark, the third country in the NATO consortium, received its first F–16 off the SABCA production line on 28 January 1980 with an initial order for 46 single-seat F–16As and 12 two-seat F–16Bs. The first units to re-equip were *Esk 727* and *Esk 730* at Skrydstrup, phasing out the ageing F–100 Super Sabres. *Esk 727*, the first to transition, was declared operational to NATO on 26 August 1981.

During the work-up, Denmark, akin to the other NATO users, had four instructors trained at Hill AFB. They then formed the nucleus of the first unit. However, unlike Holland, Denmark split the unit into two, operating the two types alongside one another and thus maintaining *Esk 727's* operational capability.

Once the Skrydstrup Wing had completed its transition it was then the turn of Aalborg and the F–104 Starfighter. *Esk 723* was the first to receive the Fighting Falcon but it was the CF-104Gs that were phased out – the MAP F-104Gs being passed to *Esk 726*. This unit in turn completed its conversion to the F–16 with the last Starfighter sortie taking place on 30 April 1986.

Norway, as the final user, drew its F–16s from the Fokker production line and had a requirement for 60 F–16A and 12 F–16B aircraft. This small force was intended to fulfil a requirement for a weapons system capable of area defence and anti-invasion strikes, but the numbers ordered were not sufficient to protect all airfields.

The *Kongelige Norske Luftforsvaret* (RNorAF) received its first aircraft on 25 January 1980 and the intention was to re-equip four squadrons. A former F–5 user, *332 Skv*, was chosen to become the OCU and was fully equipped with the F–16 by the autumn of 1981. The first operational unit was *331 Skv* at Bodo, an air defence squadron which drew its aircraft from the enlarged *332 Skv* at Rygge. The second operational unit was *334 Skv* which was Norway's anti-shipping CF-104 unit armed with the Bullpup missile, although it too had been equipped with the F–5 until the middle 1970s. Then *334 Skv* began receiving its F–16s from the second production batch, the aircraft being delivered on 26 June 1982. Following its work-up *331 Skv* traded in its early model aircraft for the latest batch, returning the former to Rygge.

The final unit scheduled to receive the F–16 was originally mooted as *338 Skv* at Orland, but it was *336 Skv* at Rygge that started to transition to the type in 1984. However in 1985 the decision was reversed and *338 Skv* became the fourth squadron although the prevailing shortage of pilots and aircraft in Norway has resulted in the unit establishment being far from acceptable.

The Export Game

In the early stages of the F–16 programme the USAF opposed early delivery commitments being made to nations outside the European consortium, with the exception of Iran. This was to avoid a shortage of aircraft and spares, the service not wanting to see any other export commitments until 1981. Nevertheless, with the downfall of the Shah, Israel was quick to gain from those aircraft already on line for Iran. This block of aircraft ran from 78–0308 to 78–0467 with the IDF taking up the initial 56 airframes, the residue being cancelled. The first five aircraft, all F–16Bs, were delivered to Ramat-David Air Base on a direct flight from Pease AFB on 2 July 1980. Israel

Left
Serving alongside the AFRES unit at Luke AFB are the F–15s of the 405th TTW and the F–16s of the 58th TFW as illustrated by this aircraft, 78-0058/LF. The 'LF' tail code stands for Luke Falcon whereas that carried by the 302nd TFS/AFRES is 'LR' for Luke Reserve. *Peter R. Foster collection*

Right
The first NATO country to operate the F–16 was Belgium, which received its initial aircraft on 23 March 1979. That aircraft, FA01, still serves with No 349 Squadron to whom it was originally issued. No 349's sister squadron is No 350, which has the Gaul's head as a squadron emblem. Here FA18 returns from Solenzara, Corsica, following a weapons detachment and wears the very attractive colour scheme devised to celebrate the unit's 45th anniversary. The 'flames' on the forward fuselage were at one time standard on the unit's CF–100 and Hunter aircraft but were carried infrequently on its former mount, the F–104 Starfighter. Also, this particular jet has received the modified tail cone consistent with later aircraft housing ECM/ESM. *Peter R. Foster*

saw the great potential of the F–16 and has gone on to order a further 20 F–16As and 148 F–16C/Ds. It is one of the few countries to use the jet in anger.

In spite of the USAF's resistance to early overseas sales, the GD team was quick to snap up sales opportunities. Egypt became the first customer after Iran and was quickly followed by Pakistan, both ordering the F–16A/B models. GD, in an attempt to attract less well-off countries, converted one of the pre-production aircraft – 50747 – to the F–16/J79 version, later redesignated F–16E, and this first flew at Fort Worth on 29 October 1980. This has, however, had virtually no effect, with interested countries being prepared to accept fewer airframes at normal production standard rather than more of a slightly inferior model.

Venezuela was the next customer to receive the F–16A. The 24 aircraft spread over two years have been used to equip *161* and *162 Esquadron Group de Caza 16* at Base Aerienne Liberator at Palo Negro. South Korea ordered 36 of the F–16C/D derivative in an attempt to up-grade its air force, the first aircraft being assigned to the 161st TFS at Teagu in 1986. This was followed by the forming of the 162nd TFS, also at Teagu, on 1 November 1987.

In Europe, Turkey concluded an agreement for the supply of 160 F–16C/Ds with GD supplying the initial 10 airframes and the rest being produced locally by TUSAS at Murted. The first GD aircraft arrived at Murted aboard a C–5A Galaxy in May 1987.

In an attempt to maintain the uneasy peace between NATO's two southern partners, Congress authorised the sale of 40 F–16Gs direct from GD to Greece with deliveries to begin at the end of 1988. This agreement was finally signed on 12 January 1986, the delay a result of arguments on offset terms.

In the Far East, Singapore was initially the only country to show interest in the F–16/J79, ordering four single-seat and four two-seat aircraft in 1984. However, following US approval for the sale of production standard aircraft to Thailand in 1985, Singapore sought and gained approval itself for an upgrade with initial delivery for 1988.

Indonesia is the final confirmed Far Eastern customer for 12 F–16A/Bs, these powered by the P & W F100/220 engine for delivery in mid-1989.

Jordan has shown considerable interest in the F–16, but if rumours of a MiG–29 sale are correct then there is little likelihood of the Fighting Falcon finding its way into Jordanian colours. Nearer home, Switzerland is looking for the Mirage III's replacement and the F–16C was one of the aircraft under consideration.

With development costs running so high for new high-technology aircraft, and the cancellation of the Lavi project, Israel is likely to purchase further F–16s, whilst the Japanese Self Defence Force has settled upon the F–16 to fulfil its FSX requirements. A total of 130 aircraft are required for the JASDF at a unit cost of $30 million, with modifications to include a larger composite construction wing with radar absorbent leading edge, stretched fuselage, ventral fins under the intake, strengthened cockpit canopy, active phased array radar and updated mission avionics and computer.

GD in its wisdom has proposed an upgraded version of the F–16 called Agile Falcon. The proposal to the USAF would involve a five-nation production programme combining two already proposed USAF propulsion and avionics upgrades complete with a larger wing and composite material components. Improvements would include better manoeuvrability and landing performance, plus greater payload and range.

A decision by 1990 would enable deliveries to commence to the participating nations – with the project directed at NATO – by 1995. Whatever the future holds, we are certain to see the F–16 as one of the most widely-used fighter types since the advent of the F–86. It will be around well into the next century.

Right
Photographed from a Utah ANG KC–135E in 1982, F–16B 78-0086/HL of the 421st TFS can be seen over the Rockies prior to a range sortie. On the port outer station are practice bombs whilst the 421st Squadron name 'Black Widows' is clearly seen in the fin band. This particular aircraft was transferred to the 58th TFW at Luke AFB shortly after this photograph was taken. *Ted W. Van Geffen/IAAP*

Far right
Another F–16B to be delivered factory fresh to the 388th TFW in 1979 was 78-0088/HL. Seen from Hill AFB's high control tower, this particular aircraft was transferred to the 58th TFW as the 388th TFW began receiving Block 15 aircraft. It has since been passed on to the 6512th Test Squadron/AFFTC at Edwards AFB where it carries the 'ED' tail code. *Peter R. Foster*

Above right
Subsequently not adopted, this experimental lizard colour scheme was displayed on 388th TFW F–16B 80096/HL during 1982. At that time the jet was operated by the 34th TFS, as conveyed by its red fin band; it is pictured here at Eglin AFB. In the background can be seen a C–141A in another scheme, almost forgotten. *Ted W. Van Geffen/IAAP*

Below right
In a more normal scheme for No 350 Squadron, BAF FB03 carries the red fin band and Gaul's head, whilst it will be noted that this particular aircraft has not been retrofitted with the redesigned tail cone. In October 1987 the conversion flight at Beauvechain was upgraded to squadron level which led to redistribution of the Wing's F–16s. As a result, both Nos 349 and 350 Squadrons received 'B' model aircraft whereas these particular machines had previously been common user and were devoid of unit insignia. *Peter R. Foster*

Left
The TCA (*Transitie en Conversie Afdeling*) at Leeuwarden was formed initially to introduce pilots into the F-16 world but later undertook conversion to the air defence role. This part of the F–16 syllabus is now incorporated in the general *Klu* F–16 conversion and therefore the TCA was de-activated on 1 March 1986. Here, with its distinctive blue badge, is F–16B J271 which has the distinction of being the only two-seater to be lost by the Royal Netherlands Air Force. *Herman J. Sixma/IAAP*

Far left
The first occasion that the Danish Air Force participated in a major UK exercise with a significant number of F–16s was 'Mallet Blow 1/83'. On that occasion *Esk 727/730* detached 10 aircraft to RAF Coltishall for the duration of what had previously been an in-house exercise. Not a country to have, in recent times, displayed more than the bare minimum in unit markings, individual identification of Danish aircraft is sometimes only possible by close scrutiny of the patch on the pilot's arm. The jets do however usually carry the squadron badge on the intake beneath the cockpit, although this particular example does not. *Peter R. Foster*

Left
The Fighting Falcon is perhaps one of the best close combat fighters in existence today. However, even the most confident F–16 pilot can be given a rude awakening by the versatile British Aerospace Hawk's superb manoeuvrability. Therefore *Klu* aircraft are regularly detached to Decimomannu to pit themselves against the RAF's ADV units, whilst both Nos 322 and 323 Squadrons set up regular detachments to RAF Brawdy for DACT with No 79 Squadron. Here J254 of No 323 Squadron can be seen being escorted back to Brawdy by XX222 and XX317. *Robbie Shaw*

Right
Holland was the second user of the F-16 in Europe. Now that the TCA at Leeuwarden has de-activated the surviving F–16Bs of Holland's initial order, J259–J271 have been re-distributed between the Wing's two squadrons bringing them back up to strength after the loss of some 10 aircraft in the 10 years of operation. Here J262/78-0262 is seen at the hammerhead prior to departure from Leeuwarden in April 1984.
Herman J. Sixma/IAAP

Far right
The Royal Norwegian Air Force became a member of the F–16 club with the delivery of 272/78-0272 in mid-1979. The first operational unit was *332 Skv* based at Rygge, which also serves as the operational conversion unit. Here 274 displays 332's fin flash at RAF Alconbury in August 1987. It will also be noticed that this aircraft has the lengthened tail housing which is built as standard on all Norwegian machines and contains a brake landing chute considered essential on the icy runways in the far north.
Peter R. Foster

Right
Impressive at any time, the snow-covered Rocky Mountains create a fabulous backdrop to these two F–16As from the 421st TFS whilst on a sortie from Hill AFB. Both the jets pictured here have gone on to see service with the reserves, 78-0039 moving down the ramp to join the 466th TFS/AFRES and 79-0294 joining the 152nd TFS, the first Air National Guard unit to operate the type. *Ted W. Van Geffen/IAAP*

Far right
South Carolina became the first guard unit to adopt the F–16A, during mid–1983. The 157th TFS traded its reliable A–7D Corsair IIs in for 24 F–16As drawn primarily from the 388th TFW and retained its familiar 'SC' code. The unit, which has regularly in the past deployed to RAF Wittering, has yet to cross the Atlantic with its Falcons but this is no doubt just a matter of time. *Peter R. Foster collection*

Far left
The 474th TFW at Nellis AFB became the first front-line F–16 Wing within the USA. It was eventually joined by the 388th TFW when it lost its training commitment, but it has fallen to the Nellis units to supply much of the European re-deployment with one of its prime forward operating locations being RAF Bentwaters in Suffolk. Here a pair of F–16As from 428th TFS 'Buccaneers' await their slot time prior to the 'Coronet Re-deploy' on 6 July 1984. *Peter R. Foster*

Above left
The first unit within the structure of the USAF to receive the F–16 Fighting Falcon was of course the Air Force Flight Test Center (AFFTC) and in particular the 6512th TS. Aircraft operating from 'Ted's place' (as Edwards AFB is often referred to) have in the past been pretty anonymous although in the last couple of years have begun receiving the 'ED' tail code. *Peter R. Foster collection*

Below left
The prime test establishment units to utilise the F–16 are those associated with the ADTC at Eglin AFB. The two prime units at this location are the 3246th TW (coded 'AD'), and the 4485th TS (coded 'OT') with whom this example operates. F–16 80-0551 is seen at Tyndall AFB in October 1982. *Peter R. Foster collection*

Far left
**Former 10th TFS, 50th TFW
mount 80-0591 was delivered
to the 134th TFS Vermont ANG
in mid-1986, which drew its
aircraft from the 388th TFW
with which this particular
airframe briefly served
following its relocation from
Hahn AB. The unit reverted to
a fighter unit from its previous
role of electronic
countermeasures training with
the EB–57B, utilising the F–4D
Phantom for a brief period.
Transition to the F–16 has
created yet another slot where
Weapon System Operators
have found themselves
without a job – a problem that
will only be relieved with the
introduction of the F–15E
Strike Eagle.** *Peter R. Foster
collection*

Left
**Seen against a very black sky
F–16A 80-0613 from the 10th
TFS, 50th TFW completes its
landing at RAF Alconbury on
21 September 1984. Many of
the 'A' model Falcons
assigned to the Wing at Hahn
were, when relocated to the
States, passed on to the Guard
units at Tucson, San Antonio
and Jacksonville.** *Peter R.
Foster*

Right
Apart from the 'Red Flag' exercises, Nellis AFB also hosts 'Gun Smoke' in which units eagerly compete for the various honours. Each command holds its own fly-off and USAFE has regularly been represented by the 50th TFW at Hahn, which provides a joint team. Here several 'A' models can be seen amongst the ordnance during the 1986 meet, the last the Wing was to undertake prior to upgrading with the heavier and more sophisticated 'C' model.
Cor de Blij via Ben Ullings

Below right
NATO countries have been regular participants in 'Red Flag' exercises following the example set by the RAF in the late 1970s. Here No 23 'Smaldeel' Belgian Air Force F–16As can be seen with RF-4Cs from the 26th TRW at Zweibrucken during one of the 1986 'Flag' exercises. *Cor de Blij via Ben Ullings*

Far right
Proving that variety is the spice of life, No 23 'Smaldeel', 10 Wing F–16A FA67 lines up with an F–4C from *Esquadron 122* of the Spanish Air Force at Kleine Brogel on 31 March 1987. NATO exchanges provide an opportunity for crews to discuss and practice tactics which prove to be mutually helpful. Spain is of course upgrading its own forces with the hi-tech EF–18.
Pieter Van Gamert via Ben Ullings

Right
No 23 'Smaldeel's' sister unit at Kleine Brogel is of course the renowned 31 'Tigers'. In this shot, taken from a struggling CM 170 Magister, all four of the 31 jets are crewed by 23 'Smaldeel' pilots. This practice is common throughout the Belgian Air Force, with aircrew being split into two flights but squadron ground personnel being drawn from the Wing; therefore one line will operate the day shift and the other the evening. The net result is an exchange of mounts. *Peter R. Foster*

Far right
Denmark phased out its ageing F–100 Super Sabres before beginning transition of its air defence F–104 Starfighters. *Esk 723* **at Skrydstrup was the first to trade in the venerable old lady to be followed some two years later by** *Esk 726.* **E596 (80-3596) is seen here at Aalborg in June 1985 set amongst the overgrown conditions which abound on most of the Danish bases.** *Peter R. Foster*

Right
E596 displays its clean lines at the Alconbury air day in 1987. With 29 squadrons operating the type within Europe it is not surprising that the display scene becomes somewhat over-populated with the type. It is interesting to watch the performance of the different pilots in an aircraft which helps even the average look like aces. *Peter R. Foster*

Far right
This fine study of J616 of 311 Squadron of the *Klu* illustrated a special scheme devised for the *Klu* 1986 open day. The Dutch Air Force has a requirement for a total of 213 F–16s to replace F–104G Starfighters and NF–5 Freedom Fighters. To date six units have fully re-equipped, leaving 313 Squadron on Twenthe under transition with 314 and 316 to follow. *Ben Ullings/API*

Far left
No 315 Squadron *Klu*'s first F–16 was this 'B' model. J653 was on loan to the unit in 1984 from No 306 Squadron prior to the delivery of the FY83 aircraft which have gone to make the unit's equipment.
Herman J. Sixma/IAAP

Left
South-East Asia still places great demands on the PACAF in participation of exercises like 'Cope Thunder', 'Cope Jade', 'Team Spirit' and 'Pitch Black'. These exercises are helping to bring together some of the smaller non-Communist countries as a viable force capable of working together to maintain stability in the region. Here the 8th TFW Commander's aircraft, 81-0728/WP, can be seen during a 'Pitch Black' exercise with RNZAF A–4 Skyhawks in the background. *Greg Meggs*

Right
As the Red Arrows with the BAe Hawk, the USAF Thunderbirds team has been a fine emissary not only for the country but also for the F–16 sales drive. The unit (which in a war role is assigned to the 474th TFW and does periodically maintain its capability) equipped with the Fighting Falcon in 1982 following the loss of four T–38 Talons in a training accident. Since equipping with the type its safety record has been excellent, something it has never attained with any other type save perhaps the F–100 Super Sabre. *USAF*

Far right
The F–16B is used extensively in the training role, but is considered by most pilots to be one of the most uncomfortable aircraft to ride back-seat due to its incredible manoeuvrability leaving even the most hardened stomach thinking of other things. Although most front-line squadrons maintain a couple of examples on strength, they serve no real purpose other than for incentive and orientation rides. These aircraft are used on normal sorties just as much as the single-seat versions – sometimes with and sometimes without the back seat being occupied. Here 81-0818 of the 10th TFS, 50th TFW lands at RAF Alconbury, with a menacing cloud formation in the background. *Peter R. Foster*

Far left
Holland's fifth squadron to re-equip with the F–16A, and final F–104 Starfighter operator, was 312 Squadron at Volkel which began the transition in 1983. The unit is equipped with the bulk of the FY81 aircraft and is easily identified by its distinctive badge consisting of a black disc with two crossed golden swords and a red lightning flash. The example depicted is 81-0871, seen at RAF Coningsby during a UK air defence exercise in October 1985. *Peter R. Foster*

Left
One of the most interesting USAF operators of the type is the 57th FWW at Nellis AFB on the outskirts of Las Vegas. The unit is responsible for the development of tactics and the operational introduction of new weapons, and serves in a similar role to the RAF's Operational Evaluation Units (OEU). The unit at Nellis operates both the A and B versions whilst Detachment II at Luke AFB is responsible for service evaluation of the F–16C and D models. Here F–16A 82-0910/WA drops away following a refuelling from a KC–135E of the Utah ANG. *Ted W. Van Geffen/IAAP*

Right
KC–135s are essential to the redeployment of US forces to Europe and the Far East, whilst they also enhance training within the US itself. They provide the photographer with an ideal photo platform, with the boom operator's position an excellent vantage point. Here 57th FWW F–16B 82-1033/WA is seen off the tanker's starboard quarter. It is carrying a centre-line fuel tank, a luggage pod on the port station and an AIM–9 acquisition round on the wing-tip rail. *Ted W. Van Geffen/IAAP*

Far right
Although it has been common practice over many years for squadron commanders to 'specialise' their aircraft, in recent times Wing commanders and Air Division commanders have followed suit and, as can be seen on this 363 TFW F–16B, 82-1041/SW, also the 9th Air Force commander. As often happens when such high-ranking officers deign to fly, it is always the specially-marked aircraft that is assigned to them. One result is that several aircraft receive such markings to ensure that one is always available. *Regent Dansereau*

Right
On the theme of special schemes, F–16A 83-1076/HS is specially marked as the 31st TFW commander's mount. The luggage pod on the outer port station carries the inscription of Col H. Hale Burr, the unit's commander. This particular Wing still operates the F–4D alongside the F–16, whilst it had the only squadron to deactivate on the type, the 306th TFS. *Don Jay*

Far right
The latest USAF Wing to equip with the F–16 is the 347th TFW at Moody AFB, Georgia. This particular aircraft, 83-1107, carries no fin code and is the commander's aeroplane. It was also drawn from the source of the last F–16As produced for the USAF and was previously assigned to the 13th TFS, 432nd TFW at Misawa in Japan. The Wing is currently still re-equipping, with many of its aircraft coming from the 8th TFW which is presently transitioning to the F–16C. *Don Jay*

Far left
The 13th TFS, 432nd TFW at Misawa, Japan, only operated the F–16A for a short period during which time it lost only one aircraft. That machine, 83-1115, is depicted here specially marked as the Wing commander's mount. Its remains currently reside on the dump at Misawa AB. *USAF*

Left
On exercise, this Dutch F–16A, J193 (83-1193) from 311 Squadron, is seen landing at RAF Lakenheath to where it had been detached for the period of the UK air defence exercise 'Priory 2/87'. It will be noticed that the aircraft also sports a red/white checkered fin stripe acquired during its detachment to CFB Goose Bay for low level training. *Peter R. Foster*

Far left
When the 86th TFW at Ramstein began its transition to the F–16C, two F–16s were adorned with special marks, the first being the 86th TFW commander's aircraft (84-1286) which received this striking red/white striped tail reminiscent of the days of the Sabre. However, unlike those days when such markings were commonplace, anyone flying this jet became a target to all the other hungry fighter jocks in Germany. *Herman J. Sixma/IAAP*

Left
The other F–16 to be specially marked at Ramstein was 84-1316 which received these marks for the commander of the 316th Air Division. Neither jet now serves with the Wing as both squadrons up-graded to GE F110-engined aircraft before operational capability was achieved. *Herman J. Sixma/IAAP*

Right

Although the engining of F–16s with the F110 began with the FY85 block of aircraft initially, aircraft within that order came off the Fort Worth production line in an either/or state with those aircraft fitted with the P & W F100 engine being assigned to the 50th TFW at Hahn AB. Here a versatile example, 85-1418/HR, is put through its paces at Alconbury during August 1987. *Peter R. Foster*

Far right

Although the 86th TFW initially received P & W F100-engined F-16Cs, the unit soon had GE F110-engined machines delivered as US policy to get away before an all Pratt & Whitney-engined force took effect. Its former F100-engined machines were gradually transferred to the 50th TFW at Hahn AB and 363th TFW at Shaw AFB in the USA. The first squadron for the 86th was originally thought to be the 417th TFS but in fact these jets were for the 512 th TFS which received a different fin tip band. The second unit was the 526th TFS, which began receiving its FY85 aircraft in late 1986/early 1987. *Peter R. Foster*

Far left
Departing RAF Alconbury at the end of its display routine, F–16C 85-1418/HR and its sister aircraft, 85-1399/HR, make an attractive paired take-off from runway 30. It will be noted that both aircraft are assigned to the 10th TFS but that the blue fin band and 'HR' tail code of '418' have gold highlights specially adopted for the USAF's 'Gun Smoke' gunnery meet held at Nellis AFB. *Peter R. Foster*

Left
Having traded in F100-engined 84-1286, the 86th TFW commander adopted 85-1426 with a revised marking. The jet is held on the strength of the 526th TFS whilst that painted for the 316th Air Division commander appears on 512th's strength. '426' appeared outside its shelter in June 1987 displaying a full load of AIM-9M Sidewinder missiles. *Peter R. Foster*

Right
Following the 432nd TFW in receiving the F110-engined F–16C is the 8th TFW at Kunsan in South Korea. By November 1987 the Wing had received eight examples and the first squadron, the 35th TFS, was expected to complete transition during January 1988. Here 86-0207/WP taxies beneath the control tower at Kunsan. *Peter R. Foster*

Far right
Whilst the 86th TFW was in transition from the F–4E Phantom to the F–16C its alert commitment was maintained by Air National Guard F–4D Phantoms under a detachment called 'Creek Party'. The Phantoms were drawn from North Dakota, California and Minnesota, remaining on alert for over 12 months whilst the crews were rotated at regular intervals. The extra length of deployment was caused by the 86th's service introduction of the F110 in the F–16. Here refuelling from a KC-135 over Germany are a pair of F–4D Phantoms and F–16D 85-1511/RS from the 526th TFS. *Ted W. Van Geffen/IAAP*

Right
The Dutch were the first of the European consortium to employ KC–135s for IFR practice and now detach to CFB Goose Bay on a regular basis for low-level training. The ground attack units have also deployed to Nellis AFB for a 'Red Flag' detachment and No 306 Squadron should have, by the time this book is published, taken part in the 1988 Reconnaissance Air Meet at Bergstrom AFB. Here nicely captured over a clear North Sea in May 1985 is F–16B J270 of No 323 Squadron.
Robbie Shaw

Far right
Engine running ... ground crew complete final checks before permission to taxi is given. Here F–16C 85-1570/MJ of the 14th TFS, 432nd TFW, is prepared for a mission at Misawa AB in November 1987.
Peter R. Foster

Far left
**Main checks complete . . .
ground crew await the Inertial
Navigation System to settle
down before waving the jet off
the pan. The same procedures
are adopted whether regular
or reserve units; here 466th
TFS F–16As prepare for a
sortie.** *Ted W. Van
Geffen/IAAP*

Left
**Pan checks complete and INS
aligned, aircraft taxi to the
'last chance' where the
armourer awaits to remove
the arming pins from the
weapons load.** *Ted W. Van
Geffen*

Right
A RNorAF pilot runs through his pre start-up checks prior to a sortie. This view illustrates well the smooth contours of the one-piece canopy. *Allan Burney*

Far right
The 401st commander's F–16A was one of the first to be seen in Europe sporting rather more attractive marks. Here the jet, 82-0977/TJ, is displayed at the Alconbury air day in 1986 wearing a high visibilty unit badge, the squadron colours around the intake and the name *El Conquistador*. *Peter R. Foster*

APPENDIX

F–16 SERIALS

Model	Serials	Notes
YF–16	72–01567–8	
F–16A	75–0745–750	50745 was F–16–101DFE, 50747 to F–16E, 50749 to F–16XL, 50750 to F–16AFTI (Listed as NF–16A in official inventory)
F–16B	75–0751–752	
F–16A	78–0001–027	
F–16A	78–0038–076	
F–16B	78–0077–115	
F–16A	78–0116–161	FMS Belgium FA01–FA46
F–16B	78–0162–173	FMS Belgium FB01–FB12
F–16A	78–0174–203	FMS Denmark E174–E203
F–16B	78–0204–211	FMS Denmark ET204–ET211
F–16A	78–0212–258	FMS Netherlands J212–J258
F–16B	78–0259–271	FMS Netherlands J259–J271
F–16A	78–0272–300	FMS Norway 272–300
F–16B	78–0301–307	FMS Norway 301–307
F–16A	78–0308–354	FMS Israel 100/102/105/107/ 109/111–114/116/118/121/124/ 126/129/131/135/138/219/220/222/ 223/225/227/228/230/232–234/ 236/237/239/240/242/243/246/ 248/249/250/252/254/255/257/ 258/260/261/264–267/269/272– 277/281/282/284/285/287/290/ 292/296/298/299
F–16B	78–0355–362	FMS Israel 001/003/004/006/008/010/ 015/017
F–16	78–0363–467	FMS Iran – cancelled
F–16A	79–0288–409	
F–16B	79–0410–432	
F–16A	80–0474–622	
F–16B	80–0623–638	
F–16A	80–0639–643	FMS Egypt 9301–9305
F–16B	80–0644–648	FMS Egypt 9201–9205
F–16A	80–0649–668	FMS Israel
F–16A	80–3538–587	FMS Belgium FA47–FA96
F–16B	80–3588–595	FMS Belgium FB13–FB20
F–16A	80–3596–611	FMS Denmark E596–E611
F–16B	80–3612–615	FMS Denmark ET612–ET615
F–16A	80–3616–648	FMS Netherlands J616–J648
F–16B	80–3649–657	FMS Netherlands J649–J657
F–16A	80–3658–688	FMS Norway 658–688
F–16B	80–3689–693	FMS Norway 689–693
F–16C	80–3694–744	FMS Israel
F–16D	80–3745–768	FMS Israel
F–16A	81–0643–661	FMS Egypt 9306–9323
F–16B	81–0662	FMS Egypt 9206
F–16A	81–0663–811	
F–16B	81–0812–822	
F–16A	81–0864–881	FMS Netherlands J864–J881
F–16B	81–0882	FMS Netherlands J882
F–16B	81–0883	FMS Egypt 9207
F–16B	81–0884–885	FMS Netherlands J884–J885
F–16	81–0899–938	FMS Pakistan (including 28 F–16As and 12 F–16Bs)

F–16A	82–0900–1026	
F–16B	82–1027–049	
F–16A	82–1050–052	FMS Venezuela 1041, 0051, 6611
F–16B	82–1053–055	FMS Venezuela 1715, 2179, 9581
F–16A	82–1056–065	FMS Egypt 9324–9334
F–16A	83–1066–117	
F–16C	83–1118–165	
F–16B	83–1166–173	
F–16D	83–1174–185	
F–16A	83–1186–188	FMS Venezuela 8900, 0678, 3260
F–16B	83–1189–191	FMS Venezuela 2337, 7635, 9583
F–16A	83–1192–207	FMS Netherlands J192–J207
F–16B	83–1208–211	FMS Netherlands J208–J211
F–16C	84–1212–318	
F–16D	84–1319–331	
F–16C	84–1332–341	FMS Egypt
F–16D	84–1342–345	FMS Egypt
F–16A	84–1346–357	FMS Venezuela 7268, 9068, 8924, 0094, 6023, 4226, 5422, 6426, 4827, 9864, 3648, 0220
F–16A	84–1358–367	FMS Netherlands J358–J367
F–16B	84–1368–369	FMS Netherlands J368–J369
F–16D	84–1370–373	FMS South Korea
F–16C	84–1374–395	
F–16D	84–1396–397	
F–16A	85–0135–141	FMS Netherlands J135–J141
F–16B	85–0142	FMS Netherlands J142
F–16A	85–0143–145	FMS Netherlands J143–J145
F–16C	85–1398–505	
F–16D	85–1506–517	
F–16C	85–1544–570	
F–16D	85–1571–573	
F–16C	85–1574–583	FMS South Korea
F–16D	85–1584–585	FMS South Korea
F–16D	86–0039–052	
F–16	86–0054–065	FMS Netherlands
F–16C	86–0066–???	FMS Turkey to at least 069
F–16A	86–0073–077	FMS Belgium FA97–FA101
F–16D	86–0191–???	FMS Turkey to at least 194
F–16B	86–0197–199	FMS Denmark ET197–ET199
F–16C	86–0207–371	
F–16C	86–1586–597	FMS South Korea
F–16B	87–0001	FMS Belgium FB21
F–16A	87–0004–008	FMS Denmark E004–E008
F–16B	87–0022	FMS Denmark ET022
F–16A	87–0046–056	FMS Belgium FA102–FA112
F–16	87–0057–068	FMS Netherlands canx
F–16B	87–0401–0404	FMS Singapore
F–16A	87–0508–514	FMS Netherlands
F–16B	87–0515–516	FMS Netherlands
F–16C	87–1653–660	FMS South Korea
F–16	88–0001–012	FMS Netherlands
F–16A	88–0016–018	FMS Denmark E016–E018
F–16A	88–0038–047	FMS Belgium FA113–FA123
F–16B	88–0048–49	FMS Belgium FB22–FB23
F–16A	89–0001–011	FMS Belgium FA124–FA133
F–16B	89–0012	FMS Belgium FB24
F–16A	89–0013–019	FMS Netherlands
F–16B	89–0020–021	FMS Netherlands
F–16A	89–0025–027	FMS Belgium FA134–FA136
F–16N	163268–281	US Navy

F–16 units

UNITED STATES

Direct Reporting Units

4485 TS	OT	F–16A	Black/white check	TAWC Eglin AFB
422 TES	57 FWW WA	F–16A/B	Yellow/black check	TFWC Nellis AFB
F–16 FWS	57 FWW WA Det II	F–16C/D	Yellow/black check	Luke AFB
64FWS	57 FWW	F–16A/B		Nellis AFB
to convert from F–5E/F to F–16A/B early 1989				
Thunderbirds		F–16A/B		Nellis AFB
318 FIS	25 AD 'TC'	F–16A/B		McChord
To convert from 18 × F–15A to 24 × F–16A late 1989				AFB

Tactical Air Command

9th Air Force

306 TFS	31 TFW ZF	F–16A/B	Yellow/ white outline	Inactive
307 TFS*	31 TFW HS	F–16A/B	Red	Homestead AFB
308 TFS	31 TFW HS	F–16A/B	Green/ white outline and name 'Wild Ducks'	Homestead AFB

Squadron	Wing	Type	Markings	Base
309 TFS	31 TFW HS	F–16A/B	Blue/white outline	Homestead AFB

306th activated on F–16 in November 1985 but de-activated on 31 October 1986 and aircraft transferred to the 308TFS

Squadron	Wing	Type	Markings	Base
61 TFTS	56 TTW MC	F–16C/D	Yellow/white outline	McDill AFB
62 TFTS	56 TTW MC	F–16A/B	Blue/white outline	McDill AFB
63 TFTS	56 TTW MC	F–16A/B	Red/white outline	McDill AFB
72 TFTS	56 TTW MC	F–16A/B	Black/white outline	McDill AFB

56TTW to begin receiving F–16C/D models late 1988

Squadron	Wing	Type	Markings	Base
68 TFS	347 TFW MY	F–16A/B	Red	Moody AFB
69 TFS	347 TFW MY	F–16A/B	Silver	Moody AFB
70 TFS	347 TFW MY	F–16A/B	Blue/white checks	Moody AFB
17 TFS	363 TFW SW	F–16C/D	White/yellow edge	Shaw AFB
19 TFS	363 TFW SW	F–16C/D	Gold/black edge	Shaw AFB
33 TFS	363 TFW SW	F–16C/D	Blue	Shaw AFB

12th Air Force

Squadron	Wing	Type	Markings	Base
4 TFS	388 TFW HL	F–16A/B	Yellow/red lightning	Hill AFB
16 TFS	388 TFW HL	F–16A/B	Blue/white check	In-active
34 TFS	388 TFW HL	F–16A/B	Red/'rams' in white	Hill AFB
421 TFS	388 TFW HL	F–16A/B	Black/red spider	Hill AFB
428 TFS	474 TFW NA	F–16A/B	Blue/white outline	Nellis AFB
429 TFS	474 TFW NA	F–16A/B	Black/yellow outline	Nellis AFB
430 TFS	474 TFW NA	F–16A/B	Red/white outline	Nellis AFB

474TFW to de-activate late 1988

832 Air Division

Squadron	Wing	Type	Markings	Base
310 TFTS	58 TFW LF	F–16A/B	Green/gold outline	Luke AFB
311 TFTS	58 TFW LF	F–16A/B	Blue/white outline	Luke AFB
312 TFTS	58 TFW LF	F–16C/D	Black/red outline	Luke AFB
314 TFTS	58 TFW LF	F–16C/D	Yellow/black outline	Luke AFB
425 TFS	58 TFW LA	F–16A/B	to convert from F–5E/F to F–16A/B late 1989	

Pacific Air Force

5th Air Force

Squadron	Wing	Type	Markings	Base
13 TFS	432 TFW MJ	F–16C/D	Black and white checks	Misawa AB
14 TFS	432 TFW MJ	F–16C/D	Black and yellow checks	Misawa AB

7th Air Force

Squadron	Wing	Type	Markings	Base
35 TFS	8 TFW WP	F–16C/D	Blue	Kunsan AB
80 TFS	8 TFW WP	F–16C/D	Yellow	Kunsan AB
36 TFS*	51 TFW OS	F–16C/D	Red	Osan AB*

* 36th due to re-equip in late 1988

United States Air Force Europe

3rd Air Force

Squadron	Wing	Type	Markings	Base
527 AS	81 TFW	F–16C/D	Red	Bentwaters

17th Air Force

Squadron	Wing	Type	Markings	Base
10 TFS	50 TFW HR	F–16C/D	Blue	Hahn AB
313 TFS	50 TFW HR	F–16C/D	Orange	Hahn AB
496 TFS	50 TFW HR	F–16C/D	Yellow	Hahn AB
23 TFS	52 TFW SP	F–16C/D	Blue/white outline	Spangdahlen AB
81 TFS	52 TFW SP	F–16C/D	Yellow/black outline	Spangdahlen AB
480 TFS	52 TFW SP	F–16C/D	Red/white outline	Spangdahlen AB
512 TFS	86 TFW RS	F–16C/D	Green and black diagonal stripes	Ramstein AB

526 TFS	86 TFW RS	F–16C/D	Black and red diagonal stripes	AB

16th Air Force

612 TFS	401 TFW TJ	F–16C/D	Blue and white checks	Torrejon AB
613 TFS	401 TFW TJ	F–16C/D	Yellow and black checks	Torrejon AB
614 TFS	401 TFW TJ	F–16C/D	Red and black checks	Torrejon AB

401 TFW will re-locate from Torrejon in 1989

Air National Guard

111 FIS	147 FIG	F–16A/B		Texas ANG	Ellington ANGB

to convert from 18 × F–4D to 18 × F–16A in 1990

114 TFTS	142 TFW	F–16A/B		Oregon ANG	Kingsley Field ANGB+
119 FIS	177 FIG	F–16A/B		New Jersey ANG	Atlantic City ANGB†
121 TFS	113 TFG 'DC'	F–16A/B		District of Columbia ANG	Andrews AFB

to convert from 24 × F–4D to 24 × F–16A in 1990

134 TFS	158 TFG	F–16A/B		Vermont ANG	Burlington ANGB
138 TFS	174 TFG 'NY'	F–16A/B		New York ANG	Hancock Field Syracuse

to convert from 24 × A–10A to 18 × F–16A mid–1989

157 TFS	169 TFG SC	F–16A/B		South Carolina Ang	McEntire ANGB
159 FIS	125 FIG	F–16A/B		Florida ANG	Jacksonville AP
160 TFS	187 TFG	F–16A/B		Alabama ANG	Montgomery AP+
161 TFTS	184 TFG	F–16A/B		Kansas ANG	McConnell AFB

171 FIS	119 FIG	F–16A/B		Michigan ANG	Selfridge ANGB

to convert from 18 × F–4D to 18 × F–16A in 1990

178 TFS	119 FIG	F–16A/B		North Dakota ANG	Fargo (Hector Field)

to convert from 18 × F–4D to 18 × F–16A in 1990

182 TFS	149 FG SA	F–16A/B		Texas ANG	Kelly AFB
184 TFS	188 TFG	F–16A/B		Arkansas ANG	Fort Smith AP+
186 FIS	120 FIG	F–16A/B		Montana ANG	Great Falls AP
194 FIS	144 FIG	F–16A/B		California ANG	Fresno AP

to convert from 18 × F–4D to 18 × F–16A in mid–1989

195 TFTS	162 TFG	F–16A/B		Arizona ANG	Tucson ANGB

+ 114 TFTS Oregon ANG due to re-equip early 1989
+ 160 TRS Alabama ANG due to re-equip spring 1988
+ 182 TFS Arkansa ANG due to re-equip spring 1988

Air Force Reserve

89 TFS	DO	F–16A/B		Wright-Patterson AFB+
93 TFS	915 TFG FM	F–16A/B		Homestead AFB+
302 TFS	944 TFG LR	F–16C/D	Yellow/red trident	Luke AFB
465 TFS	301 TFW TH	F–16A/B		Tinker AFB+
466 TFS	301 TFW HI	F–16A/B	Black and yellow diamonds	Hill AFB

+ 93 TFS and 465 TFS due to re-equip during FY88
+ 89 TFS due to re-equip during FY89

BELGIUM

1 'Smaldeel'	2 Wing	F–16A/B	–	Florennes+
2 'Smaldeel'	2 Wing	F–16A/B	–	Florennes+
23 'Smaldeel'	10 Wing	F–16A/B	Red/white diamonds	Kleine Brogel

31 'Smaldeel'	10 Wing	F–16A/B	Tiger's head	Kleine Brogel	
349 'Smaldeel'	1 Wing	F–16A/B	Blue band	Beauvechain	
350 'Smaldeel'	1 Wing	F–16A/B	Red band	Beauvechain	

+ 2 Wing is due to re-equip 1988/89

DENMARK

Esk 723	F–16A/B	Aalborg
Esk 726	F–16A/B	Aalborg
Esk 727	F–16A/B	Skrydstrup
Esk 730	F–16A/B	Skrydstrup

NETHERLANDS

306 Sqn	F–16A/B	Eagle head on blue/black	Volkel
311 Sqn	F–16A/B	Black and white eagle on blue	Volkel
312 Sqn	F–16A/B	Crossed swords/red lightning	Volkel
313 Sqn	F–16A/B	Eagle on white runway/blue disc	Twenthe
315 Sqn	F–16A/B	Light grey lion on grey disc	Twenthe
322 Sqn	F–16A/B	Blue and grey parrot	Leeuwarden
323 Sqn	F–16A/B	Archer with red tunic, black disc	Leeuwarden
TCA	F–16A/B	Blue disc	Unit inactive

NORWAY

331 Skv	F–16A/B	Red/white/blue flash	Bodo
332 Skv	F–16A/B	Black/yellow flash	Rygge
334 Skv	F–16A/B	Red/white/blue flash	Bodo
338 Skv	F–16A/B	Black flash/yellow lightning	Rygge

F–16 Losses

Date	Serial	Base	Unit
??.??.??	72–1568	–	AFFTC
09.08.79	78–0078	HL	388 TFW
01.10.79	78–0006	HL	388 TFW
25.01.80	78–0071	HL	388 TFW
10.03.80	J216	–	–
26.03.80	78.0023	HL	388 TFW
23.07.80	78–0092	HL	388 TFW
28.07.80	FA08	–	349 Sqn/1 Wing
29.10.80	78–0110	MC	56 TTW
12.03.81	FA11	–	350 Sqn/1 Wing
27.03.81	78–0105	MC	56 TTW
06.04.81	78–0013	HL	388 TFW to GF–16A
10.04.81	79–0316	HL	388 TFW
02.06.81	280	–	*332 Skv*
03.06.81	J237	–	–
29.06.81	79–0313	HL	388 TFW
17.07.81	J217	–	323 Sqn
05.08.81	78–0046	HL	388 TFW
20.10.81	J233	–	
22.10.81	FA29	–	349 Sqn/1 Wing
15.01.82	78–0048	HL	388 TFW
19.01.82	FA14	–	349 Sqn/1 Wing
19.01.82	FA35	–	350 Sqn/1 Wing
27.01.82	79–0318	HL	388 TFW
23.03.82	78–0112	–	3246 TW
12.04.82	78–0016	HL	388 TFW
04.05.82	79–0390	NA	474 TFW
11.05.82	78–0067	HL	388 TFW
20.05.82	79–0301	HL	388 TFW
20.05.82	79–0374	NA	474 TFW
09.06.82	79–0392	NA	474 TFW
16.06.82	79–0378	NA	474 TFW
06.07.82	80–0490	WP	8 TFW
08.11.82	79–0298	MC	56 TTW
01.12.82	80–0564	HR	50 TFW
15.12.82	81–0724	WP	8 TFW
27.12.82	79–0343	NA	474 TFW
12.01.83	80–0600	NA	474 TFW
19.01.83	79–0386	HL	388 TFW
20.01.83	80–0617	HR	50 TFW
31.01.83	283	–	*331 Skv*
10.02.83	80–0478	NA	474 TFW
21.03.83	J225	–	322 Sqn
05.04.83	E175	–	
26.04.83	J224	–	322 Sqn
26.04.83	J227	–	322 Sqn
10.05.83	81–0664	HR	50 TFW

Date	Serial	Code	Unit
10.05.83	FA13	–	349 Sqn/1 Wing
11.07.83	80-0627	MC	56 TTW
25.07.83	78-0113	MC	56 TTW
04.10.83	J252	–	322 Sqn
10.11.83	FA07	–	349 Sqn/1 Wing
10.11.83	FA41	–	349 Sqn/1 Wing
10.11.83	82-0925	HL	388 TFW
18.11.83	79-0390	NA	474 TFW
25.01.84	80-0595	WP	8 TFW
27.01.84	81-0730	HL	388 TFW
10.04.84	79-0313	SC	157 TFS
01.05.84	81-0745	HL	388 TFW
02.05.84	82-1045	HL	388 TFW
28.05.84	J634	–	311 Sqn
19.06.84	78-0072	MC	56 TTW
19.06.84	ET209	–	
19.06.84	ET211	–	
25.06.84	82-0971	TJ	401 TFW
19.09.84	FB16	–	10 Wing
25.09.84	80-0477	NA	474 TFW
12.11.84	82-0959	TJ	401 TFW
13.11.84	301	–	332 Skv
12.12.84	J271	–	TCA
??.??.85	82-1043	SW	363 TFW
07.02.85	79-0323	SC	157 TFS
08.02.85	81-0818	TJ	401 TFW
10.02.85	?	–	? /USAF
01.04.85	E179	–	Esk 730
01.04.85	E186	–	Esk 730
27.04.85	83-1117	SW	363 TFW
29.04.85	FA24	–	350 Sqn/1 Wing
16.05.85	79-0416	MC	56 TTW
03.06.85	J621	–	311 Sqn
03.06.85	J865	–	311 Sqn
12.06.85	303?	–	332 Skv
08.08.85	81-0750	HL	388 TFW
02.09.85	FA06	–	349 Sqn/1 Wing
22.10.85	80-0586	HR	50 TFW
01.11.85	79-0372	SW	363 TFW
15.11.85	82-0940	WA	57 FWW
15.11.85	82-1029	WA	57 FWW
11.12.85	78-0004	LF	58 TTW
12.02.86	78-0055	AD	3246 TW
27.02.86	83-1086	ZF	31 TTW
15.04.86	J629	–	306 Sqn
26.04.86.	?	–	? /USAF
13.06.86	J626	–	311 Sqn
30.06.86	FA79	–	23 Sqn/10 Wing
??.07.86	?	–	? /IDF
10.07.86	684	–	331 Skv
10.07.86	686	–	331 Skv
20.08.86	FA33	–	350 Sqn/1 Wing
11.09.86	?	WA	57 FWW
02.10.86	?	HI	466 TFS/afres (F–16A)
09.10.86	82-0998	TJ	401 TFW
09.10.86	84-1212	SW	363 TFW
10.10.86.	FA42	–	350 Sqn/1 Wing
12.11.86.	?	SW	363 TFW
17.11.86	J244	–	322 Sqn
30.12.86	?	–	? /PAF. An F–16B
22.03.87	83-1115	MJ	432 TFW
29.04.87	?	–	? /PAF. An F–16A
22.06.87	79-0385		
23.06.87	85-1424	RS	86 TFW
24.07.87	80-0597	WA	57 FWW
24.07.87	82-0912	WA	57 FWW
25.07.87	83-1149	SW	363 TFW
27.08.87	85-1517	RS	86 TFW
14.09.87	FA63	–	23 Sqn/10 Wing
15.09.87	?	–	338 Skv
17.09.87	84-1331	HR	50 TFW
19.09.87	FA52	–	350 Sqn/1 Wing
05.10.87	?	–	? /IDF
10.10.87	?	SW	363 TFW
19.10.87	85-1463	RS	86 TFW
02.11.87	84-1270	SW	363 TFW
07.12.87	E201	–	Esk 723
10.12.87	E185	–	Esk 730
17.12.87	83-1067	TJ	401 TFW
13.01.88	82-1015	TJ	401 TFW
11.02.88	J639	–	306 Sqn
20.02.88	86-0213	LR	302 TFS/afres
?.03.88	81-0766	HS	31 TTW
14.03.88	?	–	331 Skv
22.03.88	79-0397	MC	56 TTW
31.03.88	84-1389	HR	50 TFW
18.04.88	85-1462	RS	86 TFW
23.05.88	?	?	? /USAF
31.05.88	?	SA	182 TFS
04.06.88	J625	–	311 Sqn
07.06.88	81-0713	–	159 TFS
29.06.88	84-1395	HR	50 TFW
29.06.88	85-1401	HR	50 TFW
29.06.88	86-0247	SP	52 TFW
05.07.88	?	–	334 Skv

Right
**Fitted with wingtip smoke
pods, this F–16C shows off its
agility in a climbing turn whilst
the vortices off the fuselage
shows the 'g' being pulled.**
Herman J. Sixma/IAAP

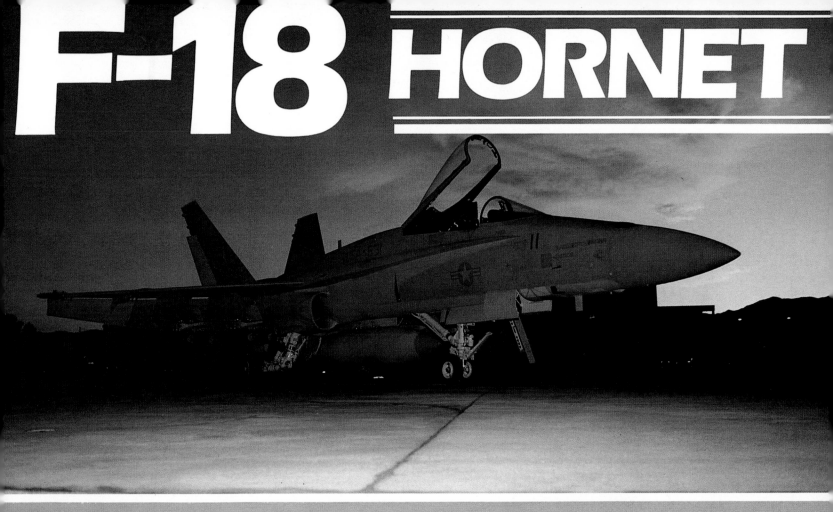

F-18 HORNET

**HERMAN J. SIXMA &
THEO W. VAN GEFFEN**

IAN ALLAN
Publishing

PREFACE

From a photographer's point of view, the trouble with the colour schemes of today's US Marine Corps and Navy aircraft is that they make for boring photographs. We look back with nostalgia to the period when the aircraft still carried bright and brilliant colour schemes. This has been particularly the case during the compilation of this album. At least when we covered the F-14 Tomcat, we could include photographs of the pre-grey and dull low-viz colour schemes. With the Hornet we could not, simply because it was not even flying operationally at that time.

To 'relieve the pain' a little bit, some (Navy) squadron commanders take the chance to paint a maximum of two of their aircraft in the traditional colourful squadron markings. And, fortunately enough, the RAAF (Royal Australian Air Force) flies its F/A-18 Hornets with traditional bright and brilliant squadron markings. In addition to Australia, Canada and Spain fly the Hornet as well (with Kuwait and Switzerland to follow), making this album not merely a compilation of Marine Corps and Navy F/A-18s.

It was tough, but fun to compile this book. We'd like to thank the following: Lt Lydia Zeller, Lt Fred Henney (both Chinfo), LCdr Gene Okamoto (NAS Point Mugu), Dennis McGrath (NAS Lemoore), Cdr Dottie Schmidt (USNR), Chief Randy Gaddo, Capt Linda Western (both USMC), the PAO Shop at MCAS Beaufort, Ken Carter (DDI), Russell Egnor (Chinfo), Capt Yves Généreux and Mr Lusignan (CAF), Greg Meggs, Peter Foster, AIR (Don Spering), Frank Mormillo, Keith Snyder and last but not least Tom Downey and Daryl Stephenson (McDonnell Douglas).

Theo W. van Geffen (IAAP)
Herman J. Sixma (IAAP)
Utrecht, Holland

Title Page:
F/A-18A (161744, EC-11)
YMFA-531 MCAS El Toro, Ca.
A 'Grey Ghost' armed with
500lb bombs ready for a dawn
MABEX support mission.
Frank Mormillo

The Hornet Story

When VFA-125, the first F/A-18 squadron in the US Navy, took delivery of its premier Hornet on 19 February 1981, a new milestone had been reached on a long and difficult road towards a new type of aircraft for the US Navy. Long, because the history of the McDonnell Douglas F/A-18 Hornet can be traced back to the Northrop P-530 Cobra, designed in the late 1960s. Difficult, because during the development and test programme, not only were serious doubts raised about its original basic design as a Light Weight Fighter (LWF), but also about the ability of one man to cope with the workload of a dual-role aircraft.

At the same time the US Air Force was also involved in selecting a new Air Combat Fighter (ACF). After its test programme and a formal evaluation at the end of 1974, it was announced on 13 January 1975 that the USAF had selected the General Dynamics YF-16 over the Northrop YF-17, although the latter type had certainly proven to be superior in several aspects. The US Navy was looking for an aircraft to replace its ageing F-4 Phantoms and A-7 Corsairs, as well as to supplement the F-14 which had become too expensive to acquire in the number originally specified. Solutions like a cheaper F-14, a navalised F-15 and improved F-4, were rejected by the Navy in favour of a new Naval Air Combat Fighter (NACF) with a secondary attack capability, designated VFAX (Fighter/Attack Experimental Aeroplane). As a result of a decision by Congress, the VFAX contest was cancelled in favour of a competition between the derivatives of the Air Force ACF contest. The prize in this NACF contest would be an order for some 800 fighter aircraft.

The two manufacturers involved in the ACF contest teamed up with other companies that could offer extensive backgrounds in the design and construction of naval aircraft: General Dynamics with Ling-Temco-Vought, and Northrop with McDonnell Douglas. The GD/LTV combination entered the competition with Models 1600, 1601 and 1602. The Northrop/McDonnell Douglas proposal, designated McDonnell Douglas Model 267, was a combination of Northrop's YF-17 navalised version, called P-630, and the first fruits of McDonnell Douglas' involvement in the NACF contest. After a series of modifications the Navy announced, on 2 May 1975, that Model 267 met the requirements best. The choice was controversial, however: the aircraft was the loser in the ACF competition and not, as Congress had supposedly proclaimed to the Navy, a version of the winner. The Navy commented that it had simply selected the aircraft most suitable to fit its needs. The prime contractor for the now called F-18 was McDonnell Douglas, with Northrop as the principal subcontractor. The construction work was split approximately 60:40. McDonnell Douglas was responsible for the forward fuselage, wings, horizontal stabiliser, landing gear, arresting hook and cockpit; and Northrop for the main structural section of the airframe including the centre and aft fuselage, and vertical fins. This workshare was to be reversed in the case of any orders being placed for a land-based version (the F-18L), to be developed by Northrop. (Iran indicated in 1976 that it was interested in buying 250 F-18Ls. This order, however, did not proceed.)

The Navy formed a team of fleet aviation and test pilots, called the Aircrew Systems Advisory Panel to evaluate systems and to provide advice to the contractors. Focuses of attention included the cockpit and the overall design of the weapon systems. One result of the Advisory Panel's attention was the addition of HOTAS (Hands-On-Throttle-And-Stick). On 21 November 1975 General Electric received a contract for the Full Scale Development (FSD) of the F404 engine, a modified YJ101 engine as used in the YF-17.

On 22 January 1976, the US Navy awarded a contract to McDonnell Douglas Corporation for FSD of the F-18. The contract also included a batch of 11 pre-production aircraft, nine single-seaters and two tandem-seaters. A first flight was scheduled to take place in July 1978. The option included 185 aircraft for the Navy and 270 for the Marine Corps in the fighter role (F-18) and 245 aircraft for the Navy in the attack configuration (A-18).

Although the name 'Hornet' had enjoyed fairly widespread use for the Navy ships of the line, Secretary of the Navy W. Graham Claytor

Left:
F/A-18C (163765, 'NH-305') 'VFA-22', NAS Lemoore, Ca
Question: What do you do when you hold an official ceremony to mark the redesignation of your squadron from 'attack squadron' to 'strike fighter squadron', and you still have no aircraft of your own? Answer: You borrow an F/A-18 from a sister squadron (VFA-113, NK-305) and with the use of paint, brushes and cardboard, paint it in your own squadron markings and then cover the original markings of the borrowed Hornet with your new ones!

This actually took place on 3 May 1990, one day before VA-22 was to be officially redesignated VFA-22, marking the end of a long period of A-7 Corsair II flying. The last A-7E was lost on 26 April 1990.

VFA-22 is still part of CVW-11. The Air Wing was last aboard USS *Enterprise* (CVN-65), but was assigned to the new USS *Abraham Lincoln* (CVN-72), after *Lincoln's* transfer to NAS Alameda, Ca, and *Enterprise's* two-year recess for a comprehensive overhaul.
Theo W. van Geffen, IAAP

Above left:

F/A-18A (163158, VM-13) VMFA-451, MCAS Beaufort, SC
The Marine Corps Air Station (MCAS) at Beaufort, South Carolina, houses six Marine Fighter Attack Squadrons (VMFA), which are equipped with the A-version of the F/A-18 Hornet. Plans for what has become the present installation were in the development stages as far back as the summer of 1941. The airport was commissioned Naval Air Station, Beaufort, on 15 June 1943.

One of the squadrons assigned to the present air station is VMFA-451 'Warlords'. The original 'Warlords' were activated at MCAS Mojave, Ca, 15 February 1944, flying F-4U Corsairs.

After a period of inactivation (10 September 1945-1 July 1946), VMFA-451 was reactivated as part of the Marine Air Reserve Training Command at NAS Willow Grove, Pa. With the outbreak of the Korean War, the squadron was called to active duty on 1 March 1951. On 1 July 1961 the 'Warlords' were redesignated as Marine All Weather Fighter Squadron — (VMF(AW)-451 — and assigned 18 F-8U Crusaders. During the following January VMF(AW)-451 completed the first transpacific flight by a single-seat aircraft, when the squadron deployed to NAS Atsugi, Japan. A new redesignation followed on 1 February 1968 when the F-8s were

traded in for F-4J Phantoms and the unit became VMFA-451. The first 'S' version of the F-4 arrived in June 1978. After departure to AMARC of the last two F-4S aircraft on 26 October 1986, conversion to the F/A-18 started, the squadron becoming operational as a Hornet unit in July 1987. F/A-18 No 500 (163133) was delivered to VMFA-451 on 15 May 1987 and received 'VM-02' markings.

The 'Warlords' were part of CVW-13 aboard USS *Coral Sea* (tailcode AK) during a 6th Fleet cruise from 31 May-30 September, 1989. VMFA-451 won the CY-90 CNO Aviation Safety Award 'S', winning the award for the third consecutive year. In early 1990 the squadron had flown 45,900hr without a major mishap, completing 12 years of accident-free flying. *Theo van Geffen, IAAP*

Above:

F/A-18A (163132, VM-01) VMFA-451, MCAS Beaufort, SC
Flying in the company of a RAF Tornado F3 over the Saudi desert, this VMFA-451 F/A-18A is equipped for CAP (Combat Air Patrol) with two AIM-9L Sidewinders and two AIM-7F Sparrows.
Sqn Ldr T. Paxton

announced on 1 March 1977 that the F-18 would be called the 'Hornet'. In December 1977 Navy test pilots based at NAS Point Mugu, Ca, tested and evaluated the YF-17 in a series of flights. Flying qualities and performance characteristics were commented upon favourably, providing a basis for confidence that the production F-18 aircraft would perform in a similar fashion.

On 17 March 1978 forward and aft sections of the first Hornet (160775) were mated at Northrop's Hawthorne facility, almost six months later followed by the roll-out of the aircraft at St Louis, Mo (13 September 1978). The first flight of the F-18 took place on 18 November 1978 with Chief Test Pilot Jack Krings at the controls. On 16 January 1979 the Hornet arrived at NAS Patuxent River, Md, to continue contractor's testing and for evaluation trials by the Naval Air Test Center (NATC). In fact, the F-18 Hornet was the first type of aircraft for the US Navy of which almost all flight-testing took place from NAS Patuxent River. This single-site testing concept allowed personnel from the Navy and McDonnell Douglas to work closely together and to ensure early implementation of any Navy comments on design. It would also enable the Navy to make hands-on assessments of the aircraft during preliminary evaluations leading up to BIS (Board of Inspection and Survey) service acceptance trials. Previous test programmes were all carried out on a variety of locations. The full-scale development testing took place through October 1982, totalling more than 3,000 test flights and 6,000 flying hours. To support F-18 test operations the NATC received additional Skywarrior tanker, Skyhawk target and Phantom chase aircraft. A North American Rockwell T-39D Sabreliner (150987) was modified to serve as a flying test-bed for the F-18's radar. Aboard the Sabreliner were the Hornet's Hughes APG-65 radar, mission computer, displays and INS (Inertial Navigation Systems), which form the core of the Hornet's airborne electronics or avionics ability. A preliminary evaluation of the radar and avionics integration was completed in July 1979. The integration received 70hr of testing aboard the T-39.

The programme also involved a number of carrier suitability trials. After a series of 70 catapult launches and 120 arrester-gear landings at Patuxent River, carrier suitability trials were carried out by the third Hornet (160777) from USS America (CV-66) in the period 30 October-3 November 1979. During the four days, 32 catapult launches and traps were made together with 17 bolters (touch-and-go landings). The first missile — a heat-seeking Sidewinder — was launched from an F-18 on 26 December 1979. The target was a radio-controlled BQM-34 drone. TF-18A No 1 (160781), the first two-seat version, arrived at NATC in December 1979, after a first flight on 25 October 1979. The TF-18 remained fully combat capable. Less than 6% of the single-place Hornet's internal fuel capacity is sacrificed for the second cockpit. A second batch of sea trials, including a series of fully automatic hands-off landings, was made in August 1982 aboard USS Carl Vinson (CVN-70) and involved 63 catapult launches and arrester-gear landings.

During the flight tests two serious accidents occurred. On 8 September 1980, Hornet T2 (160784) crashed near RAF Middle Wallop in England due to problems with the left engine. Both pilots ejected safely. Two months later, on 14 November 1980, a production aircraft (161215) crashed into Chesapeake Bay, after the pilot had lost control at about 20,000ft and ejected safely. Following this accident a spin recovery switch was incorporated to the flight computer control of all production Hornets.

The Defense Systems Acquisition Review Council (DSARC) had recommended on 8 December 1982 that the Hornet be approved for full production in the bomber role. To stress this dual role of the Hornet, the new designation became F/A-18; F/A-18A for the single-seater and F/A-18B for the two-seater. The fighter configuration had been given the Council's approval in June 1981, after which the Secretary of Defense approved full production of the Hornet on 29 June. A total of 1,157 F/A-18 Hornets have been ordered by the US Navy and Marine Corps to support both air-to-air and air-to-ground attack missions. Of this number the AO (Acquisition Objective) for the Marine Corps is 500 and for the Navy 657 aircraft. An amendment to the FY92/93 defense budget contained a request to raise this number because of inflationary reasons (for FY92 + 12 and FY93 + 28). Although the F/A-18 production was to be terminated after the FY93 lot, a supplemental request for 54 F/A-18s each in FY94/96 was approved, after which the F/A-18E/F is scheduled for production. The F/A-18 reached IOC (Initial Operational Capability) on 7 January 1983, with Marine Fighter Attack Squadron (VMFA)-314 at MCAS El Toro, Ca.

The F/A-18 Hornet in foreign service

Initially, the F/A-18 Hornet had entered service with three foreign air arms. The first country to select the Hornet was Canada. After a detailed evaluation study which started in the autumn of 1977, the competition was narrowed from six types to two: the General Dynamics F-16 and the F-18. A final decision in favour of the Hornet was announced on 10 April 1980. The contract, which was signed six days later called for 113 CF-18As and 25 CF-18B trainers to be built in St Louis, Mo. After a maiden flight on 29 July 1982, the first two production aircraft for the Canadian Armed Forces (CF-18Bs) were delivered to No 410 Operational Training Squadron at CFB Cold Lake, Alberta, on 25 October 1982. The last CF-18A was ferried to Cold Lake on 28 September 1988. All aircraft were delivered to No 410 Squadron for acceptance testing prior to allocation to other squadrons. Differences between the Canadian and US F/A-18s include the Instrument Landing System (ILS), and the addition of a 600,000 candle-power spotlight in the starboard nose section for visual identification during night interceptions. Two squadrons of CF-18s are assigned to NATO; a third squadron — No 409 — was disbanded on 25 June 1991 as part of a plan to reduce personnel stationed at Canadian Forces Europe. CF-18 aircraft and pilots from 409s were reassigned to Nos 421 and 439 Squadrons); four squadrons carry out air defence missions under command of the North American Air Defence (NORAD) and one squadron is the conversion unit; four carry out air defence duties under the command of the North American Air Defence (NORAD), and one squadron is the conversion unit.

Together with the Royal Australian Air Force, at the time of writing, the Canadians are looking at a CF-18 fatigue life management programme. Structural modifications are considered in the mid-1990s to extend the life of the CF-18 airframe into the 21st century. Although originally it was thought that the airframe would have a lifespan of 20 years, the extensive low-level performance of the CF-18 has reduced the lifetime expectation to 10-12 years.

The second country which selected the F/A-18 Hornet was Australia. The order for a total of 75 aircraft — 57 As and 18 Bs — was signed on 20 October 1981, with the first two to be manufactured by McDonnell Douglas. The remainder was to be built under license by Aero Space Technologies of Australia (ASTA) at their Avalon facility, at first from acquired MCAIR parts and later from indigenously manufactured parts. The two McDonnell Douglas-assembled aircraft were flown to RAAF Williamtown, NSW, on 17 May 1985. The first aircraft which was assembled in Australia made its maiden flight on 26 February 1985 and was subsequently assigned to No 2 Operational Conversion Unit (OCU) on 4 May 1985. The first 'all-Australian' Hornet took the air on 3 June 1985. On 16 May 1990, the 75th and last F/A-18 Hornet (A21-57) was accepted during a ceremony at Fairbairn Air Base. The year 1990

was also the beginning of a comprehensive, fleet-wide F/A-18 commonality upgrade by ASTA which will last about two years. The Australians are also interested in bringing their F/A-18As and Bs to the C and D standard. At the time of writing, the Australian Hornets equip three operational squadrons and one conversion unit.

The third export customer for the F/A-18 Hornet is Spain. In May 1983, the Spanish Government announced its plans to order 72 EF-18s (the suffix 'E' stands for España). It consisted of 60 single-seat and 12 dual-seat aircraft. The first Hornet, an EF-18B, was formally accepted by the Spanish Air Force at St Louis on 22 November 1985 and made its first flight on 4 December 1985. It was flown — together with three others — to Spain on 10 July 1986. The final two EF-18As were delivered to the Spanish Air Force on 31 July 1990. In Spain the A model is designated C15, the C standing for Caza (fighter) and the B, CF15 for Caza de Entrenamiento (fighter trainer). The aircraft are assigned to four Escuadrones (Squadrons).

The delivery of 40 F/A-18 Hornets to the Kuwaiti Air Force will take place through a FMS (Foreign Military Sales) deal. No instructions were given to stop the production after Iraq's seizure of Kuwait in 1990. At that time the aircraft were in the early stages of production. The first of 40 Kuwaiti Hornets, F/A-18D 441, rolled out at St Louis on 8 October 1991. Powered by the new F-404-GE-402 Enhanced Performance Engines.

On 3 October 1988, it was announced that a proposal to procure 34 Hornets would be submitted to the Swiss Parliament. The F/A-18 was selected in the final stages against the F-16 to fulfil Switzerland's next generation high-level interceptor requirement. In the evaluation process the Canadian Armed Forces leased a CF-18B to McDonnell Douglas (188926) in No 410 Squadron markings) which arrived in Switzerland on 31 March 1988. The contract was scheduled to be signed in September/October 1990. However, due to the changes in the European political situation, and to allow time to examine a national defence review on the 1990s, the signing of the contract was postponed. Also, in this respect, the Swiss Air Force was told to re-evaluate the Mirage 2000-5, which was offered (again), this time at 'a very interesting' price. The outcome of the examination was announced on 26 June 1991 by the Swiss Federal Military Department: 'The F/A-18 meets our military requirements to the fullest extent'. In all two finished aircraft and kits for 32 additional aircraft plus spares, technical support and training are included in the programme involving 26Cs and 8Ds.

The Republic of Korea was to have become a customer for the

Far left:
F/A-18D (441) Kuwaiti Air Force
Hornet 1044 the first in a batch of 40 F/A-18s for the Kuwaiti Air Force on the day of its roll-out on 8 October 1991. *McDonnell Douglas*

Left:
EF-18B (151-02, CE15-2) Ala 15, Zaragoza Air Base (Spain)
The second EF-18 Hornet for the Spanish Air Force, seen here in its element in the skies of Missouri. The aircraft carries the code '151-02' on the nose, denoting it will be assigned to No 151 Squadron after arrival in Spain. In 1987 the three-digit squadron code was changed to the two-wing code. *McDonnell Douglas*

A third country to prefer the F/A-18 to the F-16 Fighting Falcon was Spain making it the first Hornet customer in Europe. Although the Spanish Air Force had 144 Hornets on its wish-slip, budgetary constraints reduced the number to 72. The 72 EF-18s would replace the ageing Mirage III, the SF-5 Freedom Fighter and the F-4C Phantom aircraft in the Spanish inventory. The contract was signed on 31 May 1983, and included 60 EF-18As and 12 EF-18Bs. Some 36 aircraft would be delivered in 1986, 24 in 1987 and 12 in 1988. But because of financial difficulties, deliveries also took place in 1989 and 1990. (Eleven Hornets arrived in Spain in 1986, 26 in 1987, 15 in 1988, 12 in 1989 and eight in 1990.)

After completion of the training by McDonnell Douglas of 10 Spanish Air Force instructors, four EF-18Bs made a nonstop flight to Zaragoza on 10 July 1986. The final Spanish Hornet was delivered on 31 July 1990.

Fighter Wing 15 (*Ala de Caza 15*) was the first wing to be equipped with the EF-18. It was established at Zaragoza on 16 December 1985, but had to wait until 10 July 1986 to receive its first aircraft. The Wing's components, Nos 151 and 152 Squadrons (*Escuadrones*), each have 15 single-seaters and three two-seaters. IOC was achieved on 1 November 1988. The second Hornet wing is Fighter Wing 12, which shared Torrejon Air Base with USAFE's 401st Tactical Fighter Wing. Before converting to the EF-18, the Wing had operated the F-4C Phantom. Nos 121 and 122 Squadrons are assigned to Fighter Wing 12. The Wing still has a squadron of RF-4Cs assigned (No 124 Squadron).

Hornet as well. On 20 December 1989 it was announced that the RoKAF had selected the F/A-18 Hornet to fulfil the Korean Fighter Programme through the acquisition of 120 aircraft, the first of which would be delivered around October 1993. However, a price increase for the F/A-18s beyond the allocated budget range and a reduction in the defence budget necessitated the cancellation of the F/A-18 purchase plans. Instead a number of 120 Block 50 F-16C/D Fighting Falcons will be acquired, saving South Korea around US $1 billion.

Last July McDonnell Douglas submitted a proposal to the US Navy to sell 67 F/A-18s to Finland under a FMS (Foreign Military Sale) agreement. Technically, the US Navy will be the seller. The Finnish Air Force is looking at a follow-on aircraft for its MiG-21bis and SAAB J-35 Draken. Other aircraft in the competition are the SAAB JAS-39 Gripen, General Dynamics F-16 and Dassault Mirage 2000-5.

Finally, the IDF (Israeli Defence Force) expressed an interest in the F/A-18 Hornet, although no formal request has been received yet.

A possible contender to acquire 20 second-hand (RAAF) Hornets was the French Aéronavale. *Was*, because the French Government decided not to purchase the F/A-18 as an interim replacement for its 23 Vought F-8E (FN) Crusaders until the navalised version of the Dassault Rafale D becomes operational, but to retain its Crusaders.

From F/A-18A/B to F/A-18E/F

Deliveries of the F/A-18 Hornet to the US Navy and Marine Corps will continue in the years to come, with the improved and updated single-seat F/A-18C being the current (1991) production standard aircraft. The most important capability improvement consists of the ability to carry the AIM-120 AMRAAM (Advanced Medium-Range Air-to-Air Missile) and the infra red imaging AGM-65F Maverick air-to-surface missile. The first F/A-18C (163427) made its maiden flight on 3 September 1986 and was subsequently delivered to NATC at NAS Patuxent River on 23 September. On 22 October 1986 the first F/A-18D two-seater (163434), which is currently the production standard two-seater, made its first flight and was flown to Patuxent River. Since October 1989, all single-seat 'C' and two-seat 'D' Hornets delivered to the US Navy and Marine Corps are equipped with additional night attack systems and sensors. After the approval of the Night Attack Program in December 1984, the night attack avionics were flight-tested in early 1988 aboard prototype F/A-18D 163434. Its first fully equipped night attack test hop was made on 6 May 1988. After initial flight-testing, the aircraft was flown to NAS China Lake, Ca (Naval Weapons Center) for a seven-month test programme.

The first production night attack F/A-18C (163985) arrived at Patuxent River on 1 November 1989, while the first F/A-18D (163986) followed on 14 November. The night attack version is equipped with a new forward-looking infra red (FLIR) sensor made by Hughes Aircraft Co and called Thermal Imaging Navigation Set (TINS), designed to help pilots navigate and assist in locating, identifying and attacking ground targets at night. Two other important features include Night Vision Goggles (NVG) attached to the pilot's helmet and a colour digital moving map, displaying navigational data and vital intelligence information. Data for the map is stored on a laser disk. Within the US Marine Corps, the F/A-18D two-seater is used as a tactical aircraft, while the US Navy continues to use the F/A-18D in the traditional training role. The new night attack F/A-18Cs and Ds which are currently being delivered to the US Navy and US Marines, will continue to serve into the 21st century.

Future C and D models of the F/A-18 will have provision for the AN/ALQ-165 Airborne Self Protecting Jammer (ASPJ). When fully integrated, the ASPJ will counter the threat posed by the latest radars and missiles. They will also have enhanced engines, the EPE (Enhanced Performance Engine), which is a derivative of the F404-GE-400 engine. EPE-equipped Hornet deliveries begun in 1992. Other upgrades currently planned for the F/A-18C/D include mission computer improvements, reconnaissance capability and development of a lightweight internal cannon to replace the current M61-A1 20mm Gatling gun. The most significant upgrade, however, will be the one to the APG-65 radar, leading to the (Hughes) APG-73. A production contract was signed in June 1991 estimated at $257 million. The agreement covers the production readiness and actual production of 12 radars in the third block of FY92 F/A-18 procurement. The Canadian Forces are also participating as part of a NATO co-operative development programme. This upgrade will increase the speed and memory of the radar's signal and data processors by more than three times. Production deliveries of the APG-73 equipped F/A-18s begin in June 1994.

McDonnell Douglas is even looking further ahead and is working on an updated version of the Hornet: the F/A-18E and F/A-18F. The E and F versions grew out of a study requested by former Secretary of Defense Caspar Weinberger. Beginning in 1987 it was conducted by the Naval Air Systems Command (NAVAIR), McDonnell Douglas

Some 1½ years after Canada's selection of the F/A-18 Hornet, Australia followed, becoming McDonnell Douglas' second export customer in October 1981. The aircraft that would be replaced, after 21 years of service, was the Dassault Mirage III O/OD. As in the case of Canada, an extensive evaluation of several types took place, resulting in the selection of the Hornet. The Royal Australian Air Force (RAAF) also concluded that the Hornet's twin-engines, the excellent attrition and maintenance rates, the advanced avionics and superior performance could not be beaten by any other type in its class. Yet there was a difference: the Australians decided to licence-build the majority of the F/A-18s. The first two RAAF Hornets were manufactured in St Louis, while the initial batch of production aircraft was assembled from imported parts by Aero Space Technologies of Australia in Avalon. Australia would also build most of the F404-GE-400 engines.

As compared to the US Marine Corps/US Navy F/A-18A, the Australian Hornet has no catapult launch equipment, but it does have a High Frequency (HF) radio for long-range communications and a conventional ILS.

The two F/A-18Bs that were built by McDonnell Douglas (A21-101/102) were handed over to the RAAF on 29 October 1984. During the 15hr ferry flight to Australia, the Hornets were accompanied by USAF KC-10s and were then assigned to No 2 OCU (Operational Conversion Unit) at RAAF Williamtown, NSW, on 17 May 1985. Due to the introduction of the F/A-18, and in order to accommodate two operational squadrons and the OCU, RAAF Williamtown was extensively modernised at a cost of more than A$100 million. To control the Hornet squadrons at RAAF Williamtown, the 81st Fighter Wing was activated on 2 February 1987. The RAAF suffered its first F/A-18 casualty on 18 November 1987, when F/A-18B A21-104 crashed 40 miles Northwest of Townsville, Queensland. Double the amount of money spent at RAAF Williamtown had to be spent to refurbish RAAF Tindal, Northern Territories (NT). The base had to be rebuilt almost completely in order to house the RAAF's fourth F/A-18 unit.

Instead of the permanent Mirage presence in Malaysia, detachments to Singapore and Butterworth totalling some 16 weeks are made twice a year, the first detachment taking place in September 1988.

Below:
F/A-18A (A21-21)   No 75 Squadron, Tindal, NT
The last RAAF squadron to convert to the F/A-18 was No 75 Squadron. Until the arrival of its first Hornet in May 1988, No 75 Squadron had operated the Mirage III O/OD from Darwin, NT. The unit was PCS-ed (Permanent Change of Station) to RAAF Tindal, NT, in September 1988 and achieved IOC status on 1 October 1988.
Greg Meggs

and Northrop. Its objectives were to identify potential enhancements to the F/A-18 that would ensure it could fulfil the Navy's requirements for a versatile, affordable strike fighter into the 21st century. The study defined seven upgrade approaches for the F/A-18, of which the F/A-18E/F represents NAVAIR's preferred configuration. It builds upon several incremental upgrades, already underway for the C/D, and is based also on the improvements identified in the Hornet 2000 study. Both the single seat E and the two-seat F models will have greater range and payload performances, more powerful engines, increased carrier bring-back capabilities, and growth provisions for advanced avionics and weapons systems.

A modification to the F/A-18's airframe is the primary feature of the E/F upgrade. Structural changes include slightly longer fuselage (+ 4.1ft), and an enlarged wing (+ 100sq ft). The changes will increase the aircraft's internal fuel capacity by 3,000lb (extending the Hornet's mission radius up to 40%, depending on mission specifics.) The larger wing improves flight characteristics and includes two additional external weapons stations. Increased engine power (+ 12,000lb thrust) will be provided by F404 derivative engines. Proposed changes to the crew station include an eight-by-eight inch tactical situation display and a touchscreen up-front display. The FY92/93 budget request includes $1.4 billion for the development of the new Hornet versions. Through the extension of the F/A-18 programme the gap can be filled until an alternative for the cancelled A-12A Avenger II has been found. The first F/A-18E should fly in 1995. Initial operating capability (IOC) could be reached in 1998. It is thought that the structure of the Carrier Air Wing of the future will consist by 2010 of 42 F/A-18E/Fs and 18 AXs (replacement for the A-6), while the F-14 will be gone.

Below:
F/A-18B (A21-108)   No 3 Squadron, Williamtown, NSW
No 3 Squadron became the RAAF's first operational Hornet squadron. Before starting conversion in May 1986, No 3 Squadron had operated with 12 Mirage III O aircraft in Butterworth, Malaysia. It disbanded on 31 March 1986, giving the Mirage aircraft to the newly reformed No 79 Squadron at Butterworth, but reformed at RAAF Williamtown, NSW, one day later. Its first F/A-18 was welcomed on 30 August that same year, and arrived from No 2 OCU. The squadron has a multi-role mission, but also has a responsibility of developing F/A-18 air-to-air attacks. *Greg Meggs*

Below:
F/A-18A (A21-25)   No 77 Squadron, Williamtown, NSW
RAAF Williamtown's third Hornet unit is No 77 Squadron. It reformed as an F/A-18 unit on 1 July 1987. Before conversion, No 77 Squadron had flown the Mirage III O/OD. After also receiving No 2 OCU's Mirages, No 77 Squadron became the largest RAAF squadron since World War 2 with 43 Mirages and 16 MB326H aircraft assigned. No 77's mission was Mirage pilot conversion,

Mirage fighter combat instructor courses and Macchi introductory fighter courses. In early 1987, No 77 Squadron also received a number of Winjeels to train FACs (Forward Air Controllers). The lead-in training mission and MB326H aircraft were transferred to No 2 OCU after conversion to Hornet. Besides its normal multi-role mission, No 77 Squadron develops air-to-ground tactics.
Greg Meggs

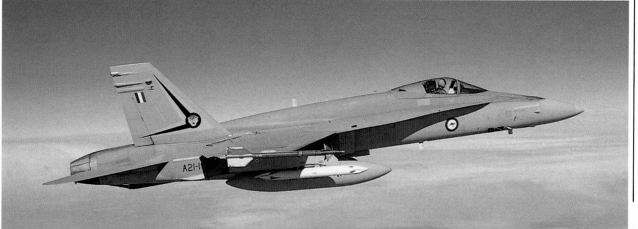

Below left:
F/A-18A (A21-1)   No 2 OCU, Williamtown, NSW
No 2 OCU at RAAF Williamtown, NSW, is responsible for the training of RAAF Hornet pilots. To accomplish this mission, the OCU has some 14 aircraft assigned. The squadron had operated as the Mirage training unit and also had been tasked with the lead-in training role in the MB326H. The mission and aircraft were transferred to No 77 Squadron when No 2 OCU stood down in December 1984. The first Hornets were received in May 1985. When No 77 Squadron converted to the F/A-18, No 2 OCU resumed its old mission of lead-in training, consequently receiving back the MB326s. However, mission and aircraft were later transferred to No 76 Squadron, also at RAAF Williamtown. *Greg Meggs*

Canada became the first export customer for the F/A-18 Hornet. The mission of the Canadian Hornet is fulfiling the air defence role within NORAD (North American Air Defence) and the tactical fighter role in support of Canada's NATO obligations in Europe. To accomplish this mission the Canadian Armed Forces possess six CF-18 squadrons, of which four are stationed in Canada (Nos 416, 425, 433 and 441 Squadrons) and responsible to Air Command's Fighter Group. The remaining two in Germany (No 421 and 439 Squadrons) are responsible to Canadian Forces Europe's 4th Fighter Wing (which is assigned to the 1 (Canadian Air Division). In a recent move to reduce personnel stationed at Canadian Forces Europe, the third Canadian Squadron (409) was disbanded on 25 June 1991 with the pilots and aircraft being reassigned to the other two squadrons. In addition, Canada-based No 410 Squadron takes care of the training of new Hornet pilots, while the Aircraft Engineering Test Establishment (AETE) also possesses some CF-18A/B aircraft. Two of the Canada-based fighter squadrons (Nos 416 and 433) are designated Rapid Reinforcement NATO squadrons and will deploy to Lahr (Germany) to reinforce NATO in times of tension, under 3 Fighter Wing.

The Hornet has replaced the CF-101 Voodoo, CF-104 Starfighter and CF-5 Freedom Fighter. One of the main reasons why the Canadians selected the Hornet was the safety aspect of a twin-engined aircraft over Canada's frozen north.

Until January 1984, when the first operational unit started the conversion to the Hornet, time was used to produce the conversion syllabus and to form the nucleus of Hornet instructors. However, the first group of pilots went through training with VFA-125 at NAS Lemoore, Ca. By the end of July 1984, deliveries of CF-18s from St Louis were suspended following the discovery of fatigue cracks in the stub attachments for the central fins. Several aircraft were grounded, while flying was severely restricted pending modifications. The result was a delay and change in the re-equipment programme. In succession, the following squadrons formed or reformed on the CF-18: No 409 'Nighthawk', No 425 'Alouette', No 439 'Tiger', No 421 'Red Indian', No 441 'Silver Fox', No 433 'Porcupine' and No 416 'Black Lynx'.

On 23 April 1990, all CF-18s were grounded for at least 48hr after the fourth accident in the course of that year involving the loss of four pilots and five Hornets. Six other CF-18s had been lost since the aircraft had been operational in 1982. Human error seemed to be the only common thread found in the mishaps, rather than any deficiency in the airframe and/or engines. In late September 1991 the Canadian Department of National Defense announced further reductions in their forces in Europe, which are in line with overall European defense cutbacks. The cuts will include the closure of Baden-Söllingen Air Base by 1994 and Lahr

Air Base by 1995, and the withdrawal of both 421 and 439 Squadrons to Canada. The 1st (Canadian) Air Division will be downgraded to an Air Group in 1992. After the return of the two units two CF-18 Hornet Squadrons in Canada will receive the 'as needed' status for deployment to Europe and use by NATO in case of a crisis.

Above right:

CF-18A (188739)   1 CAG, Baden-Söllingen AB, Germany
Until 15 June 1991 the Air Division consisted of three CF-18 units: Nos 409, 421 and 439 Squadrons. Although No 409 Squadron was planned to become the first operational Canada-based unit, the re-equipment programme had to be changed because of fin fatigue problems and a shortage of spares. Consequently the 'Nighthawks' (their motto is 'midnight is our noon') were transferred to Baden-Söllingen and replaced No 441 Squadron. Its first four CF-18s arrived on 30 May 1985. No 421 Squadron disbanded as a CF-104 unit on 1 October 1985 and was reactivated on 22 May 1986 as a CF-18 unit. No 439 Squadron reformed at Baden-Söllingen on 29 November 1985. 1AD was reactivated at Lahr on 28 May 1988, replacing 1CAG.

In this photograph two 1CAG CF-18As touch down at Kleine Brogel's runway after finishing a mission in Tactical Air Meet (TAM) 1986. *Theo van Geffen, IAAP*

Right:

CF-18A (188709)   No 410 Squadron, Cold Lake, Alberta
CF-18A (188760)   No 421 Squadron, Baden-Söllingen, Germany
A rare combination: a Cold Lake-based No 410 Squadron CF-18A in formation with a Baden-Söllingen-stationed No 421 Squadron CF-18. The 'Red Indians' became the third Canadian unit in Germany to convert to the Hornet (the name 'Hornet' is not officially accepted by the Canadians). Aircraft flown in the past by the squadron were the Spitfire, Sabre and Starfighter. *Peter Foster*

14

Right:
**CF-18As (188728 and others)
No 409 Squadron, Baden
Söllingen, Germany**
A formation of No 409
CF-18As over Southern
Germany. *Canadian Forces by
WO Vic Johnson*

Below right:
**CF-18A (188742) No 409
Squadron, Doha, Qatar**
A CF-18A of No 439 Squadron
on the taxiway at Doha ready
to take-off for CAP. It is
equipped with three 330 US
gal fuel tanks, two AIM-9
Sidewinder and four AIM-7
Sparrow air-to-air missiles.
Note the Arabic on the leading
edge root extension. Before
'Desert Storm' started the
CF-18s were on QRA; during
the operation they flew round-
the-clock missions.
Canadian Forces

After the unanimous approval of the United Nations Security Council, Resolution 661 imposed economic sanctions on Iraq on 6 August 1990. Four days later Canada's Prime Minister announced that he would contribute two destroyers and a supply ship to aid a multi-national military effort in the Gulf Region. To provide air cover for the Canadian ships and to augment the multi-national air resources already in place the Prime Minister announced on 14 September 1990 the decision to send a squadron of 18 CF-18s to the Gulf. The entire Canadian effort in the Gulf region would eventually be known as Operation 'Friction'. Qatar agreed to provide an operating base (at Doha) and facilities. The base was nicknamed 'Canada Dry'. Doha was not designed for such a large number of aircraft (USAFE F-16Cs and Qatari and French Mirage F1s were also stationed there). For this reason the CF-18s had to be parked on portable class 60 steel trackways.

Under the Canadian Air Task Group Middle East (CATGME), No 409 (Tactical Fighter) Squadron became the first Canadian unit to deploy to the Gulf on 6 October 1990. Their first CAP was flown one day later. To carry out this mission the CF-18s were equipped with AIM-7 Sparrow and AIM-9 Sidewinder air-to-air missiles in addition to the M-61 20mm cannon. While flying CAP missions, CF-18 pilots received flight control direction through specialised US Navy ships, thus reacting to direction from US controllers, an arrangement which proved very effective.

In mid-December 1990, No 439 (Tactical Fighter) Squadron relieved 409 Squadron. On 11 January 1991 the deployment of six additional CF-18s — from 416 (Tactical Fighter) Squadron, Cold Lake — was announced, while simultaneously a Boeing 707 air-to-air refuelling aircraft was deployed, to enable the Hornets to fly around-the-clock missions, and to assist in refuelling aircraft.

When 'Desert Storm' started on 17 January 1991 the role of the CF-18s was expanded to sweep and escort functions. The sweep mission consisted of air operations dedicated to establishing air superiority over enemy territory. The first two sweep and escort missions with four CF-18s per mission were flown on 21 January, although both missions were called off while the aircraft were in flight because of bad weather. One month later (20 February) the Canadian Minister of National Defence announced that CAF's CF-18s would, once the appropriate equipment was in place, undertake air-to-ground attack missions against military targets inside Kuwait and Iraq, in addition to providing CAPs for allied shipping in the Gulf. While the CF-18s from Baden-Söllingen were deployed to Doha,

Hornets from Canada augmented the units in Germany. These aircraft plus the six 416 Squadron aircraft from Doha returned to Canada on 17 and 18 March.

Canadian CF-18s had no contacts with Iraqi aircraft in the air. The only engagement with the enemy took place in late February when in the middle of the night two CF-18s were called to assist two USN aircraft which were engaging an Iraqi-Exocet-equipped TNC-45 patrol boat. The CF-18s fired a Sparrow missile which missed, but were able to hit the boat with gunfire. After a new attack by Navy aircraft the boat was sunk. In all, 34 CF-18s were deployed to the Gulf, with a maximum of 24 in theatre at any one time. The CF-18s flew 5,730hr (and the Boeing 707, 306hr). No Hornets were damaged. 439 Squadron (augmented) returned to Baden-Söllingen on 5 March 1991, until January 1993 when they returned to Canada via Prestwick. Baden-Söllingen closed on 20 January.

Additional Information:

★ On 7 December 1992 the US Navy signed a $3.715 billion development contract for the F/A-18E/F Hornet upgrade. The cost-plus-incentive contract covers $7\frac{1}{2}$ years of engineering and support activities, including the manufacture of five single-seat 'E' and two dual-seat 'F' models plus three ground test articles.

★ On 5 June 1992 the Finnish Minister of Defence signed a Letter of Offer and Acceptance in the sale of 64 F/A-18 Hornet fighters, including 57 F/A-18Cs and seven F/A-18Ds. Deliveries will begin in late 1995 and continue through 2000.

★ VMA(AW)-533 was redesignated VMFA(AW)-533 on 1 October 1992 as the 4th Marine Corps F/A-18D squadron. Before receiving their first Hornet, the unit was moved to MCAS Beaufort, SC. The other MCAS Cherry Point based A-6E units will move to Beaufort as well before converting to the F/A-18D. They are VMA(AW)-224 and 332.

★ VMFA-333 and 531 were deactivated at MCAS Beaufort and MCAS El Toro respectively on 31 March 1992.

★ VMFA-112 at NAS Dallas started conversion from the F-4S to the F/A-18A and B in the Fall of 1992.

★ VAQ-34 at NAS Lemoore will have been disestablished by 1 October 1993 with the EW agressor role going to the US Navy/Reserve.

★ VFA-127 at NAS Fallon added six F/A-18A Hornets to its fleet of 16 F-5E/Fs in 1992. The 'Desert Bogeys' mission is combat training of Hornet pilots and support of the Strike Warfare Center

F/A-18A (163166,'DR-05)   VMFA-312, MCAS Beaufort, SC
F/A-18A (163149, DR-08)   VMFA-312, MCAS Beaufort, SC
The sixth and final MAG-31 F-4S squadron at MCAS Beaufort, SC,
that converted to the F/A-18 Hornet was Marine Fighter Attack
Squadron (VMFA)-312. They became operational as a Hornet
squadron in July 1988.

   VMF-312 was commissioned on 1 June 1943 at Page Field, SC,
with 10 SNJ-4 Texans and a single F4Y-1D Corsair. After
assignment to MAG-11, receiving 24 Goodyear FG-1 Corsairs, the
'Checkerboards' operated from the captured Kadena airstrip until
the war's end. Altogether 59.5 combat kills had been accounted for.
From March-June 1951, VMF-312 flew assigned escort and
blockade missions against North Korea from the light carrier
Bataan. Some 4,945 accident-free hours of carrier operations were
amassed while logging 1,920 carrier landings. Via the F-9F, FJ-2,
FJ-3 and F-8U-1, the squadron received the F-4B in February 1966
and was consequently redesignated VMFA-312. The squadron
relocated from Beaufort to MCAS Cherry Point, NC, on 15 February
1971, but moved back south on 1 September 1974. VMFA-312 is
the oldest operational fighter squadron in the Marine Corps. In July
1990 VMFA-312 deployed for six months to MCAS Iwakuni in Japan
under the Unit Deployment Program and relieved VMFA-122 on
17 July. In its turn in April 1991 VMFA-122 relieved the
'Checkerboards', who had had to extend their stay at Iwakuri to
nine months because of the situation in the Persian Gulf. Four
months later — on 8 August — VMFA-321 received their first three
F/A-18C attack Hornets.

Left:
**Aircraft 05 is carrying an AGM-88A HARM on the pylon under the
left wing and an AIM-9L on the left wingtip launch rail. The AGM-
88A HARM (High-Speed Anti-Radiation Missile) has a higher speed,
longer range, faster reaction and a more destructive warhead than
its predecessors Shrike and Standard Anti-Radiation missiles.
Under the right wing the aircraft carries an AGM-84A Harpoon air-
to-surface anti-shipping missile. HARMs were frequently used
against Iraqi air defence radar installations and SAM sites.** *US Navy*

Right:
**It is a common practice in the Marine Corps that after returning
from a mission, aircraft make a 'hot' refuel stop before progressing
to their spot on the flightline.** *Theo van Geffen, IAAP*

Left and Above:

F/A-18A (161964, DW-03)   VMFA-251, MCAS Beaufort, SC
F/A-18A (163165, DW-12)   VMFA-251, MCAS Beaufort, SC

'*Custos Caelorum*' — or 'Guardians of the sky' — is the motto of VMFA-251 'Thunderbolts', the third squadron at MCAS Beaufort, SC, that converted from the venerable F-4S Phantom to the F/A-18 Hornet.

The first local F/A-18 flight was made by the CO on 17 June 1986 in aircraft 161965, which had been received from VFA-106, NAS Cecil Field. The 'Thunderbolts' were declared operational on 25 August 1986. For the period 1 June 1988-31 May 1989, VMFA-251 received the (USMC) Commandant's Aviation Efficiency Trophy in recognition of 'the squadron's outstanding performance in flight safety, accident prevention, combat readiness and overall participation in Naval Aviation competition'. The unit completed seven years and 30,000 accident-free flying hours on 5 April 1990.

VMFA-251 was formed in North Island, Ca, in 1944 as VMO-251. The role was reconnaissance and observation, flying the F-4F Wildcat. On 31 October 1964 the 'Thunderbolts' received the F-4B followed in June 1971 by the F-4J. Later the unit became the first Marine squadron to convert to the slatted wing F-4S.

The 'DW' unit code is carried in the inner surface of the fin, making enough room on the other surface for the distinguishing lightning flash. *Both: Theo van Geffen, IAAP*

F/A-18A (162454, VE-01)   VMFA-115, MCAS Beaufort, SC
F/A-18A (162465, VE-12)   VMFA-115, MCAS Beaufort, SC
The second Marine Corps Air Station (MCAS) to convert to the
F/A-18 was Beaufort in South Carolina. The station houses six
Hornet units, which are controlled by Marine Aircraft Group
(MAG)-31, which reports directly to 2 MAW at MCAS Cherry Point,
NC. MAG-31 has been stationed at Beaufort since 1 November
1961. Its role is to conduct anti-air warfare and offensive air
support operations in support of Fleet Marine Forces from
advanced bases, expeditionary airfields or aircraft carriers.

The 'Silver Eagles' were organised in Santa Barbara, Ca in July
1943 as VMF-115, flying the F-4U Corsair. In the Korean War,
VMF-115 flew 9,250 combat sorties. In following years transition
was made to the F-6A Skyray and VMF-115 became VMF(AW)-115.
On receipt of the F-4B in January 1964 the squadron was
redesignated VMFA-115. From October 1965 to March 1971 the
'Silver Eagles' were stationed in South Vietnam, completing 35,000

combat sorties. In July 1977 the unit was relocated from MCAS
Iwakuni to Beaufort, flying the F-4J at that time. The last flight in
the F-4S was made on 14 December 1984. Training in the F/A-18
was received at NAS Cecil Field, Fl from the Navy East Coast Fleet
Replacement Squadron, VFA-106. The first two Hornets were
received on 3 July 1985, and the C-1 status (combat ready) was
achieved on 28 January 1986. In mid-1991 VMFA-115 had achieved
30,000 accident-free flying hours.

Marine Corps units stationed in CONUS (Continental United
States) participate in the Unit Deployment Program (UDP) at MCAS
Iwakuni, Japan. Normally, two Hornet squadrons are involved and
deployed at the same time. During their six-month stay at Iwakuni,
units are assigned to Marine Aircraft Group (MAG)-15. In mid-July
1989, VMFA-115 ferried its 12 Hornets to Iwakuni and replaced
VMFA-333. VMFA-115 in its turn was replaced by VMFA-122 in
January 1990, taking over the squadron's Hornets.
Both: Theo van Geffen, IAAP

Above and Right:

F/A-18A (162398, VW-00; 163144, VW-10) VMFA-314, MCAS El Toro, Ca

Marine Fighter Attack Squadron (VMFA)-314 'Black Knights' at MCAS El Toro, Ca, was the first operational squadron in the US Marine Corps — beating the US Navy — to convert to the F/A-18 Hornet. They became operational as an F/A-18 squadron on 7 January 1983, during ceremonies at MCAS El Toro, which also marked the official start of Hornet flight operations at the station. Squadron personnel had received training since August 1982 from VFA-125 at NAS Lemoore, Ca. The first Hornet arrived on 15 December 1982.

Commissioned on 1 October 1943 and flying the F-4U Corsair, VMFA-314 was the first MAW-3 unit to convert to jet aircraft, the F-9F Panther in 1952. This was followed in October 1961 by

another 'first': it became the first Marine squadron to convert to the F-4B Phantom. In early 1966 the 'Black Knights' made the move to Da Nang, South Vietnam, where more than 28,000 combat sorties were flown.

VMFA-314 was part of Carrier Air Wing (CVW)-13 aboard USS *Coral Sea* (CV-43) between October 1985 and May 1986. In March and April 1986 the 'Black Knights' participated in actions against Libya: Combat Air Patrols (CAP) and SAM suppression missions were flown, meaning the combat début for both the Hornet and the AGM-88A HARM. VMFA-314 won the CNO aviation safety 'S' for CY-90.

The photographs show F/A-18As of VMFA-314 after flying a DACT mission against F-16A/B Fighting Falcons of Oregon ANG's 114 TFTS in late April 1990. F/A-18s from El Toro are frequent visitors to Kingsley Field, Or. *Both Theo van Geffen, IAAP*

Right:

F/A-18B (161249, 01)
USNTPS, NAS Patuxent
River, Md

The US Naval Test Pilot
School is stationed at
NAS Patuxent River, Md. The
School was established in
1958 and its task is to train
experienced Naval pilots,
Naval Flight Officers, US Army
helicopter pilots, foreign
students and engineers, to
become fully qualified test
pilots, test flight officers and
test project engineers. Some
68 graduates are produced
annually from two concurrent
classes. A class takes 11
months of instruction
consisting of specific fixed-
wing, rotary-wing and
airborne systems curricula.
Aircraft types include the A-
4M, TA-7C, T-2C and U-6A.

The photograph shows F/A-
18B of the TPS in a splendid
white and red colour scheme,
quite a contrast to the present
operational 'colours'. The F/A-
18B has proven to be
extremely useful in
demonstration of the high
angle of attack handling.

Dave Ostrowski via AIR

Above right:

F/A-18A (161925, 7T-156)   NATC, NAS Patuxent River, Md
F/A-18A (160782, 7T-151)   NATC, NAS Patuxent River, Md

Patuxent River Naval Air Station was born of an effort to centralise
widely dispersed air testing facilities established during the pre-
World War 2 years. Flight test operations started in 1942, within a
year of the first turf being dug. By the end of 1944, the Station had
formed the Service Test, Electronics Test, Flight Test and Tactical
Test Divisions. The Naval Air Test Center (NATC) was established as
a separate entity on 16 June 1945, organisationally dividing the test
and support functions. The first US test of the adaptability of jet
aircraft to shipboard operations was conducted by NATC in 1946,
when an FH-1 Phantom was flown aboard USS *Franklin D.
Roosevelt.*

A sweeping reorganisation took place in 1975. Under the plan,
Flight Test, Service Test and Weapons Systems Test Divisions were
disestablished and were replaced by Strike Aircraft, Antisubmarine
Aircraft, Rotary Wing Aircraft and Systems Engineering Test

Directorates. NATC is the Naval Air Systems Command's principal
site for development testing. The Strike Aircraft Test Directorate
(SATD) tests experimental and production fixed wing, attack, fighter
and other specifically designated aircraft, by technical analysis of
characteristics exhibited on the ground, aboard ships and in flight.
Test programmes include monitoring contractor development of
fighter and attack aircraft, support and participation in contractor
full scale development (FSD) tests. Major programme involvement
includes F/A-18, F-14B, F-14D and AV-8B. A Marine Aviation
Detachment (MAD) at Patuxent River supports the Navy and Marine
Corps' projects in the various NATC Directorates. The NATC was
disestablished by 1 January 1992 and consolidated within the
NAWC (the Naval Air Warfare Center) in a massive plan to
streamline and restructure the Navy's Research, Development, Test
and Evaluation establishments. One of NAWC's major divisions, the
Aircraft Division, is located at NAS Patuxent River. The division is
responsible for aircraft, engines, avionics and aircraft support.

Dave Ostrowski, via AIR/US Navy

Left:

F/A-18A (161366, XF-25) VX-4, NAS Point Mugu, Ca
Air Test and Evaluation Squadron Four (VX-4) at NAS Point Mugu, Ca, tests aircraft weapons systems and support equipment in the environments in which they will be used. The 'Evaluators' also develop tactics and doctrine for Fleet uses of these weapons and associated support systems. VX-4 has evaluated most of the Navy's air-launched guided missiles. The unit continues to evaluate the expanded performance capabilities of the Phoenix missile and its related weapon systems under various threat conditions. The squadron was the first Navy squadron to operate and maintain the Hornet, and has conducted the F/A-18 Operational Test and Evaluation (OPEVAL) at various test sites throughout the USA. The first Hornet was received in February 1981.

In this photograph a F/A-18A Hornet of VX-4 is readied for a launch off the first catapult aboard USS *Carl Vinson*.
Don Linn, via AIR

Left:

F/A-18A (161744, AD-323) VFA-106, NAS Cecil Field, Fl
Before VFA-106 'Gladiators' was re-established at NAS Cecil Field, Fl, on 27 April 1984 as the F/A-18 Hornet Atlantic Fleet Replacement Squadron — making the beginning of East Coast transition training of F-4 and A-7 squadrons to the Hornet — all Hornet–related training of pilots and aircraft maintenance personnel for both the US Marine Corps and Navy had been carried out at NAS Lemoore, Ca, by VFA-125.

The 'Gladiators' were originally established as Fighter-Bomber Squadron 17 in January 1945. After completion of combat operations in Korea, the squadron was designated Attack Squadron 106. VA-106 was involved in the catastrophic fire aboard USS *Forrestal* on 29 July 1967, which destroyed or damaged over half of the squadron's A-4 Skyhawks. The unit was disestablished on 7 November 1969. The 'Gladiators' achieved several milestones, including the achievement of over 80,000 accident-free flying hours in early 1990, and the attainment of an unparalleled 100% pilot qualification.

VFA-106 has 60 F/A-18s assigned, including the C and D model. The squadron was the first Fleet Training Squadron to receive the F/A-18C.

This photographs shows a VFA-106 F/A-18A being pushed back manually during carrier qualifications aboard USS *America*.
Don Spering, AIR

Above:

***F/A-18A (162871, AG-305) VFA-136, USS** Dwight D. Eisenhower*
When the USS *Dwight D. Eisenhower* (CVN-69) departed Norfolk, Va,
on 8 March 1990 to relieve the USS *Forrestal* in the Mediterranean
for a routine deployment, its Carrier Air Wing Seven included two
types of aircraft in their first major deployment: the S-3B Viking
with VS-31 and the F-14A (Plus) since redesignated F-14B with
VF-142 and VF-143.

The deployment was to become a very dramatic one. The carrier
participated in the evacuation of foreign nationals from war-
plagued Monrovia, Liberia. Just after the invasion of Kuwait by Iraq
the 'Ike' received orders to sail through the Suez Canal to the
Persian Gulf. The ship returned to Norfolk, Va, on 12 September
1990 after having been relieved late in August by USS *Saratoga*.
The Hornet components of CVW-7 are VFA-131 'Wildcats' and
VFA-136 'Knighthawks'. VFA-136 was established at NAS Lemoore,

Ca on 1 July 1985. The 'Knighthawks' made the move to Cecil Field
in March 1986 and joined CVW-13 three months later. It made its
first cruise from 29 September 1987 to 29 March 1988. Since then,
VFA-131 and 136 joined CVW-7 aboard the 'Ike'. The 'Knighthawks'
were the 1989 winners of the Cecil Field Silver Bombs award for
air-to-ground excellence. On 10 April 1990, Lt-Cdr Randy Causey of
VFA-136 recorded the one millionth flying hour of the F/A-18. The
achievement comes just seven years after the Hornet reached
operational capability with the Navy in March 1983, and combines
flying hours for all F/A-18 operators, including NASA. Lt-Cdr
Causey, who recorded his 1,000th Hornet flying hour, had been
launched from USS *Dwight D. Eisenhower* in the Mediterranean.

CVW-7's two F/A-18 units traded their As in for the C model,
after returning from their 1990 trip. The 'Knighthawks' received
their first C on 13 November 1990. *US Navy (Lt-Cdr John Leenhouts)*

Left:

F/A-18As (161523, One; 161520, Two; 161521, Three; 161524, Four) 'Blue Angels', NAS Pensacola, Fl

The US Navy Flight Demonstration Team 'Blue Angels' gives some 75 shows every year, completing some 125,000 miles. Since the formation of the team in 1946, more than 210 million people have watched the 'Blue Angels'. Although its home station is NAS Pensacola, Fl, quite a bit of time is being spent at NAS El Centro, Ca, to undertake pre-season work-up training. To accomplish its mission, the 'Blue Angels' have nine F/A-18s assigned, eight F/A-18s and a single F/A-18B. The As are numbered 1-6, 8 and 9, and the B number 7. The single-seaters are frequently re-numbered throughout the demo season. The aircraft — early production F/A-18s with the gun removed — are no longer suitable for carrier operations. They are equipped with civilian ILS and navigation equipment, a smoke generating system and new flight control system software, optimised for aerobatics. The announcement of converting from the A-4F to the F/A-18 was made on 24 February 1986. The changeover to the Hornet marked the 17th consecutive year in which the US Navy has flown McDonnell Douglas-built aeroplanes in the 'Blue Angels' squadron. The first 'Blue Angels' F/A-18 was modified by McDonnell Douglas, the remainder by NARF (Naval Air Rework Facility) at North Island. Training in the aircraft started in January 1987 at NAS El Centro. The first airshow using the F/A-18 was given on 25 April 1987. The squadron was renamed Navy Flight Demonstration Squadron on 1 December 1973. *Frank Mormillo*

Right:

F/A-18A (161366) 'Blue Angels', NAS Pensacola, Fl
F/A-18A Six, one of the two solos, performs during the open house at NAS Miramar in August 1988. The wing surfaces are partly covered by condensation vapour.
US Navy (PH1 Bruce R. Trombecky)

Above:

F/A-18D (163434) McDonnell Douglas Corp, St Louis, Mo
This photograph shows the prototype of the F/A-18D Night Attack Hornet making a test flight along the banks of the Mississippi river. The first flight of the type (there is no difference in designation as to Ds, with or without night attack capabilities) was made from the company's airfield in St Louis on 6 May 1988. The delivery to the Navy of the first production Night Attack F/A-18 took place on 1 November 1989, the receiver being NATC (Naval Air Test Center) at NAS Patuxent River, Md, for further evaluation. The US Navy will use the twin-seat F/A-18s as trainers, although the Ds are delivered to the Navy with two stationary hand controls to operate the weapons systems. These are used by Marine Corps backseaters instead of the stick and throttle; a modification kit is provided to the Navy allowing the installation of conventional flight controls in the rear cockpit.

The F/A-18D will also be used by the US Marine Corps, which will re-equip its VMA(AW) squadrons with the type, transferring the A-6E Intruders to the US Navy. The D version of the Hornet will also

replace the RF-4B Phantom and the OA-4/TA-4 Skyhawk. The type provides the MAGFT (Marine Air-Ground Task Force) with a platform capable of tactical reconnaissance and tactical air control, while retaining the offensive and defensive anti-air capabilities of the F/A-18A and C. Initially, the MC wanted 48 F/A-18Ds, but this number was later raised to 72. The first unit to receive the new aircraft was VMFA(AW)-121 'Green Knights' at MCAS El Toro on 11 May 1990. *McDonnell Douglas*

Above:

The cockpit in Night Attack F/A-18C and two-seat D model Hornets has three multipurpose colour display screens, including a colour digital moving map, and an improved head-up display. Images from the aircraft's forward-looking infra-red navigation sensor are projected on to the head-up display and allow pilots to see through the dark. Through a minor (software) upgrade and the addition of beacon mode bombing, the F/A-18D is receiving an all-weather close-support capability. *McDonnell Douglas*

Above:

F/A-18A (162890, NF-202) VFA-151, USS Midway

VFA-151 is one of the only two US Navy F-4 units which converted to the F/A-18 Hornet. In that process, VF-151 was redesignated VFA-151 on 17 June 1986. Strike Fighter Squadron 151 was originally commissioned Fighter Squadron 23 in 1948 at NAS Oceana, Va. In February 1959, VF-23 became VF-151. Five years later the 'Vigilantes' converted to the F-4 Phantom and made a total of seven cruises to Yankee Station in the Gulf of Tonkin. During the seventh cruise (aboard USS *Midway*), VF-151 spent 205 days in combat operations, flew over 2,500 sorties and delivered nearly three million pounds of ordnance.

On 30 June 1973, CVW-5 and its units moved to NAF Atsugi, Japan, which would be used as its forward deployment base. In September, VF-151 and its sister squadron VF-161, exchanged their F-4Ns for the F-4Js which were received from VF-191 and 194 when the USS *Coral Sea* returned to Alameda, Ca. From the F-4J the squadron converted to the upgraded F-4S. In 1988 the 'Vigilantes' completed 32,000 accident-free flying hours over a period of eight years.

Before CVW-5's Strike Fighter force returned to NAF Atsugi in October 1986, the squadrons deployed to NAS Fallon, NV, for an intensive training programme. VFA-151 departed NAS Lemoore on 17 November 1986. Refuelled by US Air Force KC-10 and KC-135 tankers, the trip took the 'Vigilantes' to the Far East via NAS Barbers Point, Hi, and NAS Agana. When *Independence* replaced *Midway* as forward-based carrier in Yokusuka on 25 August 1991, VF-151 stayed on *Midway*. The 'Vigilantes' arrived back at NAS Lemoore on 11 September 1991 and were assinged to Commander, Strike Fighter Wing, US Pacific Fleet until assignment to CVW-2 and USS *Constellation*. The first deployment is not scheduled unitl spring 1993. *Mike Grove via AIR*

Carrier Air Wing 14 (CVW-14) aboard the USS *Constellation* was the first Air Wing to deploy with the F/A-18 Hornet. It was also the first ever deployment of a carrier with F-14 Tomcats and Hornets, making the wing the most modern and powerful one in the world. The CVW's Strike Fighter components comprise VFA-25 and VFA-113, the US Navy's first deployed F/A-18 squadrons. The 'Stingers', originally designated as VF-113, formed in July 1948, flying the F-4U Corsair. After conversions to the Cougar and Panther, VF-113 was redesignated VA-113 in March 1956 and re-equipped with the A-4 Skyhawk. The year 1965 brought the 'Stingers' to combat in South East Asia, flying the A-4C from the deck of USS *Enterprise.*

In December 1968 the unit converted to the A-7 and completed six combat cruises in South East Asia as part of CVW-2 aboard the USS *Ranger.* The US Navy's Strike Fighter era began on 25 March 1983 when VA-113 was redesignated VFA-113. The last mission with the A-7E was flown on 23 March 1983. The first F/A-18A was received by the 'Stingers' on 16 August 1983 and the transition was completed on 14 December 1983.

The 'Stingers' last mishap occurred in 1974 when the squadron was flying the A-7E Corsair II. It meant the start of the longest accident-free streak in the history of Navy and Marine Corps tactical aviation, running in September 1991 to an unbelievable 17.5 years and 76,000 flying hours, of which 36,000 have been with the Hornet. In 1989, VFA-113 won the Chief of Naval Operations Safety Award, Safety 'S'. During that year's cruise aboard USS *Constellation,* the squadron flew over 4,300hr and logged more than 1,300 carrier landings, all without a single mishap.

CVW-14's last combat deployment was made on board USS *Independence* (CV-62). The *'Indy'* sailed on 23 June 1990 on what should have become a routine deployment to the Western Pacific and Indian Ocean, but in August the Iraqi invasion of Kuwait changed these plans considerably. The ship received orders to sail to the Gulf of Oman and stayed on station for three months. On 1 October *Independence* entered the Persian Gulf for a training exercise. This was the first time a US carrier did so since USS *Constellation* in 1974. Relieved by the USS *Midway, 'Indy'* began the long trek home on 2 November 1990.

VFA-113's sister squadron in the Wing is VFA-25 'Fist of the Fleet'. The squadron is a veteran command in naval aviation. It was commissioned in 1943 as Torpedo Squadron 17 and operated the SB2C attack bomber; through VA-6B and VA-65 it became VA-25 in July 1959. The unit flew the A-1 Skyraider until April 1968, when it started conversion to the A-7B. Four of VA-25's A-1s made history on 20 June 1965, when they shot down a North Vietnamese MiG-17 while on a ResCap mission without fighter protection. The A-7E was received two years later and the type was flown through the spring of 1983. At that time the first VA-25 pilots began training on the F/A-18. Redesignation to VFA-25 followed on 1 July 1983. The full complement of 12 aircraft was reached by March 1984. In mid-1987, VFA-25 had accumulated 55,000 accident free flying hours in a 12-year period. During the December 1988-June 1989 deployment on board the USS *Constellation,* the 'Fists' were awarded their second consecutive Battle Efficiency 'E' award and the CNO Safety 'S' award. In addition VFA-25 also received the Capt Michael J. Estocin award for 1988. This also gave VFA-25 unprecedented acknowledgement as the 'Triple Crown' winner for the US Navy Strike Fighter community.

After arriving home on 20 December 1990 the squadron did not stand down, but emphasised combat readiness through flying an increased number of sorties in preparation for a possible departure to the Gulf region. On 11 September 1991 the 'Fists' and the 'Stingers' arrived at NAS Lemoore and prepared themselves to convert to F/A-18Cs, with a night strike capability. VFA-113 received its first F/A-18CN on 18 October, VFA-25 followed two weeks later. Eventually CVW-14 will be assigned to USS *Carl Vinson* (CVN-70).

Above right:
F/A-18s (161936, -307; -305; -306)   VFA-113, USS **Constellation.** *McDonnell Douglas*

Right:
F/A-18A (NK-300)   VFA-113, USS **Constellation** NK-300, sporting the colours of its Air Wing Commander, refuels from a KA-6D of VA-196. *Naval Aviation News*

Left:
F/A-18A (161939, NK-400)   VFA-25, USS Constellation.
McDonnell Douglas

Below:
F/A-18A (161942, NK-403) VFA-25, USS Constellation.
Frank B. Mormillo

Left and Above:

***F/A-18A (163126, AC-303) VFA-15, USS** Theodore Roosevelt*
***F/A-18A VFA-15, USS** Theodore Roosevelt*

The 'Valions' will celebrate their 50th anniversary on 10 January 1992, making them one of the oldest squadrons in the US Navy. They were established as Torpedo Squadron Four (VT-4) aboard USS *Ranger* on 10 January 1942 flying the SBD Dauntless. Other aircraft flown since its inception were the TBM Avenger, AD-4 Spad and A-4. Transition to the Skyhawk was made between August and November 1965, although original plans had called for a transition to the A-6 Intruder. Via the A-7B in June 1969, the E model of the Corsair II was received in October 1975. While embarked aboard USS *Independence* in November 1980, VA-15 saw extensive sea-going action, while on station off Lebanon during the Israeli-Syrian missile crisis. Three years later the 'Valions' were back in the region, this time as a part of the multi-national Peace Keeping

Force. On 4 December 1983, the unit made a successful air strike against Syrian targets in Lebanon. The last A-7E mission was flown on 25 August 1986. Redesignation from Attack Squadron to Strike Fighter Squadron took place on 1 October 1986. The first Hornet was received in January 1987. One month later the 'Valions' received Cecil Field's 100th F/A-18 (c/n 163124, AC-302).

The year 1990 marked the sixth consecutive year with zero mishaps, equating to 21,000 accident free flying hours. Also 1990 marked the fourth consecutive year the 'Valions' won the Light Attack Wing One dive bombing derby. The USS *Theodore Roosevelt* received orders in December 1990 to deploy with its Carrier Air Wing to the Red Sea to supplement the carriers already in the area. After the outbreak of hostilities against Iraq in January 1991, aircraft of CVW-8 became heavily involved in striking at Iraqi positions in both Kuwait and Iraq. *Both McDonnell Douglas*

F/A-18C (163465, AB-314) VFA-82, USS America
F/A-18C (163461, AB-410) VFA-86, USS America

The Strike Fighter component of CVW-1 aboard USS *America* consists of Strike Fighter Squadrons (VFA)-82 and 86. When not at sea, the squadrons are stationed at NAS Cecil Field, Fl, and managed by CLAW-1 (Commander Light Attack Wing One) who, in turn, reports directly to the Commander Strike Fighter Wings Atlantic.

VFA-82's history goes back to 1 April 1944, when it was established as Fighter Squadron 82 based at NAS Atlantic City, NJ. At that time the unit flew F6F Hellcats. VF-82 was disbanded on 15 April 1959. On 1 May 1967 it was reformed as Attack Squadron 82, flying 12 A-7As as part of CVW-6 aboard USS *America*. After one year of training, the 'Marauders' deployed to the waters of South East Asia and participated in air strikes against North Vietnam. In August 1970, conversion to the A-7E began. After returning from its final deployment aboard USS *Nimitz* with CVW-8 in June 1987, VA-82 converted to the F/A-18 on 6 November 1987, becoming the first Fleet Squadron to receive the C model. VA-82 was redesignated VFA-82 on 13 July 1987 and in February 1990 it flew west as part of CVW-9 (Composite) to escort USS *Constellation* around the Horn of South America to SLEP in Philadelphia, Pa. During the deployment, the 'Marauders' were informed that they had won the Battle 'E' award.

VFA-86 traces its origins to the Korean War. In the early 1950s, Fighter Squadron 921 was stationed at NAS St Louis, Mo. While deployed to Guantanamo Bay, Cuba, in 1953, the squadron was redesignated as VF-84. Two years later a further redesignation to VA-86 followed after transition to the F7U-3M Cutlass. On 1 June 1967, VA-86 became the Fleet's first operational A-7A squadron. Over the years, VA-86 has received six COMNAVAIRLANT Battle 'Es'. On 1 July 1987 the unit was officially redesignated VFA-86.

Arriving in the Red Sea on 16 January 1991, USS *America* brought the number of carriers in the area to four. Aircraft of the wing participated in the massive air strikes against Iraqi targets in Kuwait and Iraq flying 3,000+ sorties. The carrier returned to Norfolk, Va on 18 April. *Both McDonnell Douglas*

the largest aviation unit in the Navy. VA-125 trained over 700 A-7A/B/C FRPs and 5,500 FMPs. With the introduction of the Hornet into the US Navy, Fighter Attack Squadron 125 was commissioned as the first dual mission squadron at Lemoore on 13 November 1980. For this occasion, F/A-18A c/n 161216 had been specially painted as NJ-501. Before commission, the initial cadre of VFA-125 had been an integral part of the F/A-18 fleet introduction team. Factory training of 20 pilots had commenced in January 1981. Each pilot received extensive academic instruction by McDonnell Douglas instructors in system operation and 10hr of hands-on training in the F/A-18 design simulator, which was available prior to the delivery of the aircraft. VFA-125 was the first of three planned F/A-18 Strike Fighter Replacement Squadrons. Before the Marine Corps started its own Hornet training, personnel were trained at Lemoore. Hence the fact that the CO of VFA-125 was from the Navy and the Executive Officer from the Corps. The right fuselage of VFA-125s Hornets shows Marine Corps markings, and the left side Navy markings.

The first F/A-18A was received on 19 February 1981 (from VX-4), while the first F/A-18B arrived on 10 March 1981. In March 1983 VFA-125's name changed to Strike Fighter Squadron, reflecting the increased capability that the Hornet provides to the Carrier Air Wing. By March 1985, VFA-125 had amassed over 30,000 flying hours in the F/A-18, all accident free. VFA-125 averages some 1,500 flying hours monthly in the A, B, C and D models of the Hornet, and trains approximately 120 pilots and 3,500 maintenance crews each year. Pilots from the US Navy, US Marine Corps, Canadian Armed Forces, Royal Australian Air Force and Spanish Air Force have been trained by VFA-125. Kuwaiti AF pilots also receive training at NAS Lemoore. Operations at Lemoore are supplemented with air-to-air and air-to-ground training detachments to MCAS Yuma, Az, and NAS Fallon. *McDonnell Douglas*

Above:

F/A-18A (161748, NJ-511) VFA-125, NAS Lemoore, Ca
The entire Strike Fighter Community of the Pacific Fleet falls under COMLATWINGPAC (Commander, Light Attack Wing, US Pacific Fleet), which is located at NAS Lemoore and also encompasses NAS Alameda, Ca, and NAS Fallon, Nv. It exercises functional command of the West Coast F/A-18 Fleet Readiness Squadron, VFA-125 'Rough Raiders'.

VA-125 was disbanded on 1 October 1977 after almost 20 years of service as the backbone of the Light Attack Community on the US Pacific coast. Its mission had been the combat readiness training of Fleet Replacement Pilots (FRP) and Fleet Replacement Aircraft Maintenance Personnel (FMP). Until the introduction of the A-7A Corsair II on 25 September 1969, VA-125 flew all the models of the A-4 Skyhawk. During this period the squadron had over 100 A-4s and 1,000 officers and enlisted personnel assigned, making it

Right:

F/A-18B (161704, NJ-533) VFA-125, NAS Lemoore, Ca
On this photograph, taken from the Landing Signal Officer (LSO) platform, a VFA-125 F/A-18B is about to catch one of the wires aboard the deck of USS *Carl Vinson* (CVN-70) during carrier qualification. Note the empty back-seat. Navy two-seat B and D training Hornets are used solely by the two Fleet Replacement Squadrons, VFA-106 at NAS Cecil Field, Fl, and VFA-125 at NAS Lemoore, Ca. *Don Linn, via AIR*

Below:

F/A-18A (ND-505) 161756 VFA-305, NAS Point Mugu, Ca
The second F/A-18-equipped unit within CVWR-30 is VFA-305 'Lobos', stationed at NAS Point Mugu, Ca. Its relationship with the Hornet started on 18 January 1987, when Attack Squadron 305 was redesignated Strike Fighter Squadron 305, receiving its first F/A-18 eight days later. VFA-305's mission is to maintain full combat readiness at all times so that in case of a national emergency it could be called up to join the Naval Air Forces of the Pacific and Atlantic Fleets.

Commissioned as Attack Squadron 305 on 1 July 1970 at NAS Los Alamitos, Ca, the squadron began its operations flying the A-4C Skyhawk. In January 1971, after transferring to NAS Point Mugu, the 'Lobos' traded in their A-4s for the LTV A-7A on 26 June 1972. VA-305 operated the Corsair II for 15 years, which included a transition to the A-7B in 1978. The highlight of 1988 was the

'Lobos'' first F/A-18 carrier qualification trials aboard USS *Constellation*, which culminated in the squadron's outstanding success in deploying with CVWR-30 aboard USS *Enterprise*. In early 1991, VFA-305 surpassed 54,000 consecutive accident-free flying hours, amassed in more than 14 years of flying

The 'Lobos' were part of CVW-11 (Composite) on board the USS *Abraham Lincoln* (CVN-72), when the carrier departed Norfolk, Va on 25 September 1990 on its 22,000-mile transit around South America to its new homeport Alameda, Ca arriving on 20 November 1990. The squadron's detachment consisted of six F/A-18s, 13 pilots and 154 maintenance/administrative personnel. The Hornets participated in two major air wing strikes against Chilean airfields. The 'Lobos' won the Golden Tailhook award for the cruise. VFA-305 replaced VA-22 and 94 while these units converted from the A-7E to the F/A-18C. *Frank B. Mormillo*

Above:

F/A-18A (161735, ND-301)   VFA-303, NAS Lemoore, Ca
Like its sister Carrier Air Wing Reserve on the East Coast, CVWR-30 at NAS Alameda, Ca, has two F/A-18-equipped Strike Fighter Squadrons assigned: VFA-303 at NAS Lemoore, Ca, and VFA-305 at NAS Point Mugu, Ca.

As had happened in April 1971 with the introduction of the A-7 Corsair II into the US Naval Reserve, the 'Golden Hawks' became the first US Navy Reserve unit to convert to the F/A-18 Hornet, receiving the majority of its aircraft from VMFA-531. In this respect it had been redesignated as VFA-303 on 1 January 1984, making the move to Lemoore at the same time, and had received its first Hornet on 19 October 1985. The transfer of F/A-18s to the USNR was part of a plan to introduce more modern aircraft in the Reserve forces.

The squadron was originally commissioned at NAS Alameda, Ca, on 1 April 1970 and equipped with the A-4C, although its history dates back to 1945 when a Naval Reserve Group was organised at Livermore, Ca. In 1948, when the Group was divided into squadrons, the unit was designated Attack Squadron 876, flying the F-4U Corsair and afterwards the F-2F Banshee. VA-303 traded in its A-7As for the B model in 1978 and lost its last A-7B in October 1983, awaiting the arrival of the F/A-18 Hornet. Organisationally and operationally, VFA-303 — like other USNR units — closely parallels active duty fleet squadrons with training requirements that include all phases of combat strike fighter tactics and carrier operations.

In this respect VFA-303 together with the other units of CVWR-30 spent two weeks in August 1990 on board the USS *Nimitz* during Active Duty Training (ADT). The mission for the Air Wing units was to learn to operate and function as a single unit. The 'Golden Hawks' made some 190 traps and accumulated a similar number of flying hours. VFA-303 has recently accumulated 47,020 accident-free flying hours over a 16-year period. *Theo van Geffen, IAAP*

The National Aeronautics and Space Administration's (NASA) Ames Research Center at Dryden Flight Research Facility, Edwards AFB, flies six F/A-18As and one F/A-18B, which are on a long-term loan from the US Navy. The first Hornet was received in October 1984 and the final one in December 1989. Most aircraft were drawn from the pre-production and early production F/A-18s. Five As and the B model are used as chase and support aircraft and pilot proficiency training, replacing the F-104s. The Hornets are better qualified for the agile close-support work than the Starfighter.

The first F/A-18 received by NASA (840/160780) is used in the High Angle of Attack (HAOA) Program. 'Angle of Attack' (or 'Alpha') is an engineering term for the angle of an aircraft's body and wings relative to its actual flight path. The ultimate aim of the programme is to allow a HAOA of at least 70° through a thrust vectoring system, resulting in increased manoeuvrability, and in making high-performance aircraft safer to fly. The first phase of the study commenced in 1986 and involved more than 100 research flights at up to 55° angle-of-attack. The second phase started in the late summer of 1990, and continued through until the end of the summer of 1991.

Bottom left:
F/A-18A (840/160780) NASA, Edwards AFB, Ca
This photograph taken in March 1990 shows NASA's first F/A-18A Hornet 840/160780 being prepared for a landing at Edwards AFB, Ca. It has just completed a research mission in a programme to study the air flow over the aircraft during high angles of attack in order to validate computer codes and wind tunnel results. *NASA*

Above left:
F/A-18A (843/161250) NASA, Edwards AFB, Ca
The flightline at the Dryden Flight Research Facility shows F/A-18A 843/161250 and F/A-18B 845/160781. A glycol-based liquid, released through very small holes around the nose of the Hornet, aids researchers in flow visualisation studies; 843 shows the airflow pattern at about 30° of attack. *NASA*

Facing page:
F/A-18A (840/160780) NASA, Edwards AFB, Ca
In the HAOA research programme, smoke generators and yarn tufts are used on NASA's F/A-18A 840/160780. The aircraft is at about 30° angle of attack. The HAOA programme is conducted jointly with NASA's Langley Research Center. *NASA*

Left:
F/A-18C (163706, 64) PMTC, NAS Point Mugu, Ca

The Pacific Missile Test Center is the Navy's primary facility for air-launched weapons. Other missions include Fleet operations support and training, and electronic warfare projects. PMTC was originally established at NAS Point Mugu, Ca, as the Naval Missile Test Center.

PMTC's Sea Test Range comprises a fully-instrumented 35,000sq mile area about 125 miles by 250 miles long. To carry out its mission, PMTC has a fleet of more than 50 aircraft, many uniquely configured. These include types, such as the F-14 Tomcat, F/A-18 Hornet, RC-12M, EP-3A and RP-3A Orion. PMTC also maintains the largest and most varied inventory of airborne and surface targets in the US Navy, including the QF-4N and QF-86F. It was disestablished on 1 January 1992 when the Navy's RDT&E establishments were streamlined and restructured as a part of a new Command, the NAWC. The NAWC reports to Commander, Naval Air Systems Command and was organised in two major divisions. They are the Aircraft Division, primarily responsible for aircraft, engines, avionics and aircraft support and located at NAS Patuxent River, Md, and the Weapons Division located at NAS Point Mugu primarily responsible for aircraft weapons and weapons systems, simulators and targets. The Weapons Division has operating sites at NAS Point Mugu, China Lake, Albuquerque and White Sands, NM. *Theo van Geffen, IAAP*

Above:

F/A-18C (163738, WT-03)   VMFA-232, Shaikh Isa, Bahrain

At the time of writing, the US Marine Corps possesses four Marine Fighter Attack Squadrons (VMFA), which are equipped with the C version of the F/A-18 Hornet, including VMFA-212, VMFA-232 and VMFA-235. The squadrons are all stationed at MCAS Kaneohe Bay, Hawaii and assigned to Marine Aircraft Group (MAG)-24. In its turn, MAG-24 is assigned to the First Marine Expeditionary Brigade (MEB). Established in the Philippines in 1901, the Brigade relocated to Kaneohe Bay in 1953. The mission is to provide trained, combat-ready air-ground forces capable of executing amphibious assault or other such operations whenever and wherever directed. MAG-24 provides the air support and also comprises five helicopter squadrons, flying CH-46 and CH-53 helicopters.

Before conversion to the F/A-18, the three squadrons flew the F-4S Phantom. The first squadron to lose its Phantoms was VMFA-212 in September 1988. Pilots of the 'Lancers' started training at MCAS El Toro and maintenance personnel headed for NAS Lemoore, Ca. Two months later, VMFA-232 'Red Devils' sent their F-4S aircraft into retirement and began their Hornet orientation. Finally, the 'Death Angels' of VMFA-235 lost their last (and the last active-duty Marine Corps) F-4S on 3 February 1989.

VMFA-212 became operational as an F/A-18C squadron in February 1989, VMFA-232 in May 1989 and VMFA-235 in September 1989, receiving its final two Hornets on 13 November 1989. In connection with the build-up in Operation 'Desert Shield', the three MCAS Kaneohe Bay-based units were deployed to the Gulf area. VMFA-235 deployed on 20 August 1990 and together with VMFA-314, 333 and 451 it was assigned to MAG-70, which was established as initial controlling authority. *US Marine Corps*

Below:

F/A-18C (164030, NG-400) VFA-147, USS Nimitz
During the 2 September 1988-2 March 1989 Westpac/Indian Ocean deployment of USS *Nimitz* (CVN-68), Carrier Air Wing 9's (CVW-9) Attack Squadrons, VA-146 and VA-147 took along their mainstay — the A-7E Corsair II — for the last time. After their return to NAS Lemoore, Ca, the two squadrons started conversion to the F/A-18C Hornet. Their updated A-7s were sent to the remaining A-7 squadrons and Fleet Readiness squadrons.

For about six months, the squadrons were dispersed with personnel going to schools. In a normal training schedule no more than 10% of the squadron's personnel are at school. During conversion it will be upwards of 50% of the maintenance people and pilots in training. VFA-147 was the first Fleet Squadron ever to be commissioned at NAS Lemoore. On 1 February 1967 the

'Argonauts' of VA-147 were also the first A-7A squadron to be formed in the Pacific Fleet and first to deploy in the new aircraft. During the summer of 1969 the unit converted to the A-7E and made the first combat deployment in that aircraft. VA-147 was redesignated VFA-147 on 20 July 1989, with delivery of the first F/A-18C beginning in December. On 3 April 1990, some 30,000 mishap-free flying hours were reached. The USS *Nimitz* and its embarked CVW-9 left the US West Coast on 25 February 1991 to sail to the Persian Gulf area and returned home on 24 August 1991.
McDonnell Douglas

Above:

F/A-18D 164022, VK-06   VMFA(AW)-121, Shaikh Isa, Bahrain
The decision to re-equip the Marine Corps All-Weather Attack Squadrons (VMA[AW]) with the F/A-18D night attack Hornets was based on two reasons: a shortage of A-6E Intruders in the fleet, and to accelerate the reduction of the variety of different types of aircraft in the Marine Corps. In this respect the Hornet would replace the A-6E, OA-4M, RF-4B and TA-4F. The re-equipment plans call for the acquisition of 72 F/A-18Ds of which 48 can be equipped with the Advanced Tactical Reconnaissance System (ATARS), one Marine A-6E squadron converting per FY. Also, that MAG-11 units at MCAS El Toro, Ca, will convert first, while MAG-14 A-6E units at MCAS Cherry Point, NC, participate in the Unit Deployment Plan rotation to MCAS Iwakuni, Japan. The transitions would be conducted by VMFAT-101 at El Toro.

The first A-6E unit at El Toro to be redesignated Marine All-Weather Fighter Attack Squadron (VMFA[AW]) was VMA(AW)-121,

emphasising the advent of a new role for the 'Green Knights', the fighter role. (Eventually, the squadron will also be tasked with the photo reconnaissance role.) Redesignation took place on 8 December 1989 and the first aircraft was received on 11 May 1990. The first training class of F/A-18D aircrews, consisting of six pilots and seven Weapons System Officers (WSO) started in February 1990. Barely eight months after receiving their first F/A-18D the 'Green Knights' were ordered to deploy to the Gulf region. One of the missions was replacing the vulnerable OV-10 Bronco (two Marine Corps OV-10s were lost early in the conflict to Iraqi groundfire) as Forward Air Control (FAC) aircraft and reinstituting the 'Fast FAC' concept employed during the war in SEA. The F/A-18D played a key part in the air and ground phases of the war in the Gulf, identifying fixed and moving enemy targets, day and night, directing other aircraft into position to attack the enemy targets. *McDonnell Douglas*

Left and Right:
F/A-18C (163505, AA-406) VFA-81, USS Saratoga
F/A-18C (163508, AA-401) VFA-81, USS Saratoga
Although during 'Desert Storm' USS Saratoga's CVW-17 flew the smallest number of combat missions (2,600+) of the six participating air wings (in comparison: Ranger's CVW-2 flew 4,200+ missions), it played a prominent role in ousting the Iraqis from Kuwait. The Wing's VFA-81 'Sunliners' shot down two Iraqi MiG-21 'Fishbeds' on 17 January 1991 — the Navy's first combat kills (initially it was announced that the Iraqi aircraft involved were MiG-29 'Fulcrums') validating the strike-fighter concept. The aircraft (163508/AA-401 flown by Lt-Cdr Mark Fox and 163502/AA-410 flown by Lt Nick Mongillo) were directed to their targets by an E-C2 Hawkeye (159107, AA-600) of Sara's VAW-125. When Fox and Mongillo received the bandits call they were part of a flight of four Hornets tasked with dropping four 2,000lb MK84 bombs each on an airfield in Western Iraq. After shooting down their MiG-21s with an AIM-9 Sidewinder (Fox) and AIM-7 Sparrow (Mongillo) the pilots switched back from the air-to-air to the air-to-ground mode and continued their mission.

However, VFA-81 also had the distinction of losing the Navy's first aircraft in combat. The F/A-18C (163484/AA-403) was hit by a SAM on 17 January. The pilot, Lt-Cdr Michael S. Speicher, was killed in action. (CVW-17 also lost one A-6E and an F-14B through enemy groundfire.) On 11 March, the USS Saratoga commenced redeployment to its homebase Mayport, Fl arriving on 28 March. The units of the air wing arrived one day earlier at NAS Oceana, Norfolk, and Cecil Field. During the deployment — 217 days at sea and 20 days in port CVW-17 flew 12,500 sorties totalling 33,000 flight hours. Squadrons flew 2,694 combat missions and delivered 4,047,000lb of ordnance on enemy targets.

VFA-81 was established on 1 July 1955 as an all weather fighter interceptor squadron flying the F9F-8 Cougar. Via the A-4 Skyhawk and A-7B Corsair, the 'Sunliners' converted to the 'E' version of the A-7 in February 1970, becoming the first East Coast recipient of the type. In the last three years of A-7E operation, the squadron won the ComNavAirLant Battle 'E'. After completing its 24th Mediterranean deployment (on board the USS Forrestal) VA-81 was redesignated VFA-81 on 4 February 1988 and started conversion to the F/A-18C. In early August 1990 VFA-81 deployed for the first time since 1987. *USAF by SRA Chris Putman/McDonnell Douglas*

52

Below:

F/A-18A (162826, XE-34) VX-5, NAS China Lake, Ca

Air Test and Evaluation Squadron (VX)-5 is a tenant at NAS China Lake, Ca, operating out of Armitage Field. The squadron is part of the Operational Test and Evaluation Force, Norfolk, Va. Its mission is to conduct extensive tests of ordnance and aircraft equipment and to develop and evaluate aircraft weapon tactics. Flight-testing includes tests at all stages of weapon system development, as well as final test and evaluation of air-to-ground weapons, rockets, bombs, weapon components and control systems, flares and similar devices. The 'Vampires' were commissioned on 18 June 1951 as Air Development Squadron Five at NAS Moffett, Ca and were equipped with nine AD-1 Skyraiders. In July 1956 the squadron was redesignated Air Test and Evaluation Squadron and moved to China Lake to take advantage of the outstanding weapon-delivery facilities. In 1962 VX-5 became the first squadron to receive the A-4E Skyhawk, while Detachment Alpha was assigned two A-6A Intruders to evaluate the advanced weapon system. On 23 December 1967 delivery of the new A-7A Corsair II was made at VX-5. Testing and evaluation included all available weapons and nuclear configurations, and all manoeuvre tactics.

In 1981 the squadron aircraft inventory increased to 20 aircraft, with an addition of several Hornets for the evaluation of the type. January 1991 found VX-5 deployed to NAS Fallon, Nv with 14 airplanes and 300 personnel for two weeks. The purpose of the squadron deployment was to develop F/A-18 LOT XII night strike/fighter tactics, to ensure all aircrew were tactically proficient and to exercise the mobility of the squadron. Strike packages were flown in support of Operations 'Desert Shield' and 'Desert Storm'. To carry out its mission VX-5 flies a variety of aircraft including the A-6E, EA-6B, AH-1W and AV-8B. *US Navy by PH3 Robert C. Foster*

Above:

F/A-18A (161734, MF-00) VMFA-134, MCAS El Toro, Ca
Marine Corps Reserve flying units are organised within MAW-4, with headquarters at NAS New Orleans, La. F-4 and A-4 squadrons are continuing the transition process to the F/A-18 aircraft currently being used by active forces. The first Marine Corps Reserve unit to be equipped with the F/A-18 Hornet was VMFA-134 at MCAS El Toro, Ca conversion from the F-4S Phantom starting on 5 May 1989 with the arrival of the first Hornet. Full complement was received by August 1989.

VMA-142, stationed at NAS Cecil Field, Fl became the second unit to convert to F/A-18. The unit was redesignated VMFA-142 on 21 December 1990. VMFA-321, at NAF Andrews, Md (holding a ceremony on 13 July 1991 to mark the retirement of their F-4S aircraft) and VMFA-112, at NAS Dallas, Tx (F-4S) will transition to the F/A-18 in FY92 and FY93 respectively.

MF-00, the squadron commander's aircraft, is pictured on 29 July 1989 on final approach to NAS Dallas, Tx. *Keith Snyder*

Left and Below:
F/A-18B (162870, SH-10)   VMFAT-101, MCAS El Toro, Ca
F/A-18C (163713, SH-135)   VMFAT-101, MCAS El Toro, Ca
When Marine Aircraft Group (MAG)-13 relocated on 1 October 1987 from MCAS El Toro, Ca, to MCAS Yuma, Az, Marine Combat Crew Readiness Training Group (MCCRTG)-10 had been disbanded one day earlier. The Group's Marine Fighter Attack Training Squadron (VMFAT)-101, flying the F-4S Phantom, was PCS-ed (Permanent Change of Station) to El Toro to become the Marine Corps F/A-18 Hornet Fleet Replacement Squadron while assigned to MAG-11. Until the move of VMFAT-101 to El Toro, Hornet Pilots were trained by VFA-125 at NAS Lemoore, Ca, and VFA-106 at NAS Cecil Field, Fl. The 'Sharpshooters' were commissioned at MCAS Yuma on 3 January 1969, and were temporarily attached to MAG-33 at MCAS El Toro. VMFAT-101 was awarded the Robert M. Hansen award in October 1983, presented to the most outstanding fighter squadron in Marine aviation. When the last US Navy F-4 training squadron was disbanded on 1 June 1984, VMFAT-101 took on responsibility for training pilots and RIOs of the US Navy, becoming the sole unit in the sea services actively training crews for the F-4 Phantom. VMFAT-101 operates all versions of the Hornet. It had accumulated 50,000 accident free flying hours over a five-year period in late 1990.

An F/A-18B and an F/A-18C of the 'Sharpshooters' are pictured on finals to NAS Dallas, Tx. After a short period of carrying two-digit numbers, the squadron resumed carrying three-digit numbers.
Both: Keith Snyder

capable rates exceeded 90%. The Hornets flew a total of more than 11,000 sorties, encompassing some 30,000 flight hours. 18,000,000lb of ordnance were dropped, involving 15 different types of weapons, including some 250 HARMs. 6000+ targets were attacked — including 24 main bases, 30 dispersal bases, command and control facilities and surface-to-surface missiles. The F/A-18s were 91.5% mission and 90.4% full mission capable. The aircraft of VFA-81 and 83 accumulated an average of 128.5 flight hours.

NAS Squantum, Ma was the official birthplace of VFA-83, originally Naval Reserve Fighter Squadron 916. Via NAS Oceana, the 'Rampagers' moved to NAS Cecil Field, Fl in 1966 and were the last to fly A-4s on board the USS *John F. Kennedy*. VA-83 transitioned to the A-7E, which was flown through 1987. On 1 March 1988, the 'Rampagers' became Strike Fighter Squadron 83, flying the 'C' model of the F/A-18 Hornet.   *US Navy by CW02 Ed Bailey*

Right:
F-18A (163099, AJ-406) VFA-87   USS Theodore Roosevelt
When 'Desert Storm' was initiated in the early hours of 17 January 1991, six aircraft carriers were present in the region: The USS *Ranger* and *Midway* in the Persian Gulf and the USS *America*, *Saratoga*, *John F. Kennedy* and *Theodore Roosevelt* in the Red Sea. The *Roosevelt* had left Norfolk on 28 December 1990 with CVW-8 embarked, arriving on station in the Red Sea on 14 January 1991. One week later the carrier moved in to the Persian Gulf region. During 'Desert Storm' aircraft of CVW-8 flew more than 4,200 sorties, dropping 4,500,000lb of ordnance on targets in Kuwait and Iraq. The squadron lost an F/A-18A on a combat mission on 5 February 1991, which was not attributed to hostile action. The pilot of the Hornet, Lt Robert J. Dwyer, was killed. After the cease-fire with Iraq, the USS *Theodore Roosevelt* moved to the Mediterranean and participated in Operation 'Provide Comfort'. Through air patrols and reconnaissance, aircraft of its air wing provided security to Kurdish refugees, fleeing from Iraqi forces. The carrier arrived home on 28 June 1991.

VFA-87 was officially established at NAS Cecil Field, Fl as Attack Squadron VA-87 on 1 February 1968 while attached to VA-174 and became fully operational in June 1968. The 'Golden Warriors' were the first East Coast squadron to fly the A-7B. Transition to the A-7E was commenced on 11 August 1975. After completing flight operations in the A-7E in March 1986, VA-87 became the first of the original fleet attack squadrons at NAS Cecil Field to convert to the F/A-18A Hornet. Redesignation to strike fighter squadron took place on 1 May 1986. VFA-87s first deployment was made aboard the USS *Theodore Roosevelt* as temporary member of CVW-1.
US Navy by PHC Denis Kesue

Above:
F-18C (163509, AA-300)   VFA-83 USS Saratoga
CVW-17s second strike fighter squadron on board the USS *Saratoga* during 'Desert Storm' was VFA-83, the 'Rampagers'. Although overshadowed by the successful downing of two Iraqi MiG-21 'Fishbeds' by VFA-83's sister squadron VFA-81, the 'Rampagers' participated significantly in the strike sorties flown by sea-service pilots against carefully planned targets — including anti-air defenses and ballistic missile launchers. On 30 January all 18 F/A-18Cs of CVW-17 delivered 100,000lb of MK83 1,000lb bombs on Iraqi positions in Kuwait, the largest amount of bomb tonnage carried in a single mission. There were more than 210 US Navy, Marine Corps and Canadian F/A-18s in 'Desert Storm'. Full-mission

58

Below:
F-18D (164224, DT-00) VMFA(AW)-242   El Toro, Ca
On 14 December 1990 VMA(AW)-242 at MCAS El Toro, Ca became the Marine Corps second squadron to convert from the A-6E Intruder to the F/A-18D Night Hornet and consequently received the new designation VMFA(AW)-242 (Marine All Weather Fighter Attack Squadron). In all 60 F/A-18Ds will replace a similar number of A-6Es in five VMA(AW) units, one squadron converting per year, while 12 F/A-18Ds will be received by VMFA(AW)-225 which was re-established on 1 July 1991. VMFA(AW)-242 was originally activated as Marine Torpedo Bombing Squadron 242 on 1 July 1943 at El Centro, Ca. After operations from inland bases on Espirtu Santo, Tinian, Iwo Jima and Guam VMTB-242 returned to the USA and was deactivated on 23 November 1945. On 1 October 1960 the squadron was reactivated as Marine Attack Squadron VMA-242 at MCAS Cherry Point, NC flying A-4 Skyhawks. Returning from a tour of duty at MCAS Iwakuni, Japan, the squadron was re-established at MCAS Cherry Point and redesignated VMA(AW)-242, becoming

the first Marine Corps squadron to be equipped with the A-6A Intruder.

From 1 November 1966 to 8 September 1970 the 'Bats' flew 16,783 combat missions out of Da Nang Air Base, South Vietnam, delivering 85,990 tons of ordnance in North and South Vietnam and Laos. On 12 September 1970 VMA(AW)-242 arrived at MCAS El Toro to become the first A-6 equipped squadron in the Third Marine Aircraft Wing. In September 1977 the squadron transitioned to the A-6E and three-and-a-half years later VMA(AW)-242 started conversion to the A-6E (TRAM). In August 1983 the 'Bats' became the first Marine squadron to deploy to the African continent as part of Operation 'Eastern Wind 83' in Berbera, Somalia. VMA(AW)-242 frequently deployed to MCAS Iwakuni as part of the six-month Unit Deployment Program. On 21 December 1990 the squadron transferred its and El Toro's last A-6 Intruder to VA-52, while two months later (25 February 1991) their first F/A-18D was received.
Keith Snyder

Right:

F/A-18As of USMC enroute to Persian Gulf area

At the beginning of 'Desert Storm' more than 80% of the total Marine Corps air assets were deployed in South West Asia (SWA). Aircraft included AV-8B, EA-6B, KC-130T, OV-10B and F/A-18, helicopters included AH-1W, CH-46E and CH-53E. In total 241 fixed-wing and 325 rotary-wing aircraft were deployed, flying some 18,000 sorties. With its 241 aircraft the Marine Corps possessed 7% of the allied fixed-wing aircraft number, providing approximately 11% of the tactical fixed-wing sorties flown by all allied forces, and approximately 43% of those sorties flown by all US Naval air forces.

Included in the number of 241 Marine Corps fixed-wing aircraft were 84 F/A-18 Hornets: 12 F/A-18Ds, 36 F/A-18Cs and 36 F/A-18As. These aircraft flew a total of 5,047 'Desert Storm' sorties. The 84 F/A-18s were assigned to seven different squadrons: VMFA(AW)-121, VMFA-314 from MCAS El Toro, Ca respectively with F/A-18D and A; VMFA-333 and 451 from MCAS Beaufort, SC with F/A-18A and VMFA-212, 232 and 235 from MCAS Kaneohe Bay, HI with F/A-18C (leaving no Hornets there). The parent unit in the Gulf was MAG-11, which also included A-6E Intruders of VMA(AW)-224 and 533, EA-6B Prowlers of VMAQ-2 and KC-130F Hercules of VMGR-252, all from MCAS Cherry Point, NC, VMGR-352 from El Toro with KC-130F Hercules, and Det. VMGR-452 from Stewart AB, NY with130Ts, and was assigned to 3MAW. The Wing — provisional, as its flag was not moved, but stayed at El Toro — was the aviation combat element for the overall First Marine Expeditionary Force, 1 MEF. The deployment of Marine Corps F/A-18s was initiated on 20 August 1990, when VMFA-314 and 235 left their respective homestations. VMFA-333 and 451 left for the Gulf region one day later. Initially the squadrons were assigned to MAG-70 at Shaikh Isa, Bahrain. The Group was deactivated on 3 September when MAG-11 took over responsibility.

On 12 December VMFA-212 and 232 arrived at Shaikh Isa, one month later (14 January 1991) followed by the F/A-18Ds of VMFA(AW)-121. After the start of 'Desert Storm' the mission of the Hornets was expanded and included close air support, strike escort, battlefield air interdiction, offensive and defensive air-to-air missions and suppression of enemy air defenses. No combat sorties were missed due to maintenance problems. 95% of all sorties scheduled were completed. F/A-18As of VMFA-333 needed only 3.73 maintenance manhours per flight hour, while flying 884.7 hours.

The Marine Corps suffered no F/A-18 combat losses, but lost two aircraft in non-combat operations. On 9 March two F/A-18Cs collided in mid-air over Saudi Arabia. Both pilots ejected and landed safely by parachute. Three Hornets were damaged by SAMs and

one by AAA, but they returned safely and the aircraft were back in service within 48 hours. (One of the aircraft was hit in both engines and flew 125 miles to its homebase for recovery.)

Redeployment was initiated on 24 March with the return home of VMFA-314, followed by VMFA-333 and 451 (1 April), VMFA-232 and 235 (2 April) and finally VMFA-212 and VMFA(AW)-121 (15 May).

USAF by SSgt Scott Stewart

Below:

F/A-18A(R) (161214) McDonnell Douglas, St Louis, Mo
An F/A-18 Hornet with reconnaissance equipment made the first flight from St Louis, Mo, on 15 August 1984. During the 1hr flight, the handling qualities and performance of the recce equipment were tested. To allow the aircraft to accomplish the mission, the 20mm M61A1 gun and ammo-drum were temporarily removed and replaced by a reconnaissance equipment pallet. Return to a full fighter/attack capability was expected to take place in less than eight hours. Originally, the recce installation was tested aboard the first Hornet built, 160775.

After approval of the recce provisions in May 1987, the Systems Engineering Test Directorate at NATC, NAS Patuxent River, Md, developed a recce version of the Hornet designated the F/A-18(R). It is the second production F/A-18, c/n 161214. Testing was carried out at NAS Patuxent River, and was designed merely to determine whether the F/A-18 would be a suitable platform for a

reconnaissance mission. A recce-capable F/A-18D (D1, 163434) suited to carry the Control Data Corporation ATARS (Advanced Tactical Reconnaissance System) is to start flight testing at NAS Patuxent River, Md in January 1992. The ATARS is a digital sensor suite and comprises of low and medium altitude electro-optical sensors, an infrared sensor, tape recorders and data link. The ATARS will be installed in place of the nose gun. The Marine Corps Acquisition Objective is 31, although this number was later increased to 48. Of the first 31 ATARS the last two are expected to be funded in FY95. IOC is scheduled for FY94. *McDonnell Douglas*

Right:

F-18A (160778, 4) McDonnell Douglas, St Louis, Mo
When this photograph was taken in March 1980 of the No 4 pre-production aircraft (160778) flying over the river front in St Louis, Mo, McDonnell Douglas still talked about the development of the F-18 in two versions. The fighter escort to replace the F-4, and the light attack aircraft to replace the A-7.

As of 22 April 1991 1,000 Hornets have been delivered to the US Marine Corps, US Navy, Canada, Australia and Spain, accumulating more than 1.2 million flight hours. The number 1,000 was the 72nd F/A-18D (164237), part of Block 33 and one of 84 Hornets the Navy ordered in FY89. It was assigned to VMFA(AW)-242 at MCAS El Toro, Ca (as DT-03), the second Marine Corps A-6E unit to convert to the F/A-18D. The mission capable rate for the F/A-18 is above 80%. The July 1989-June 1990 maintenance manhours per flight hour (maintainability) was 25.5 for F/A-18 operational USMC/USN squadrons compared to 44.8 for the A-7E and 62.4 for the F-14A. The July 1989-June 1990 mean flight hours between failure (reliability) as 2.0 for the F/A-18, 0.9 for the A-7E and 0.5 for the F-14A. The F/A-18 USMC/USN loss rate as of 1 August 1990 was 4.7/100,000 flight hours (of which 1.4 were aircraft-related). A total of 22 USMC/USN Hornets were lost in the first USMC/USN) 500,000 flight hours. (In comparison: 111 A7s and 95 F-4s were lost.) The loss rate dropped to 4.52 based on 796,000 flying hours and 36 losses. Ease of maintenance is one of the other advantages of the Hornet. The ability to do one complete engine change in as little as two hours on the F/A-18, and have the aircraft on the catapult, compares with at least six hours needed for the A-7E.

The Marine Corps is continuing to develop and refine the expeditionary qualities of the Hornet. Concept development is underway to conduct F/A-18 operations from FOBs (Forward Operating Bases) in much the same manner as the AV-8B. When married up with new, portable arresting gear, the Hornet will be capable of operating from expeditionary surfaces less than 2,000ft long.

APPENDIX

Unit	Code	Name	Type	Replacing/ Converted from
US MARINE CORPS				
MCAS Beaufort, SC		MAW-2/MAG-31		
VMFA-115	VE	Silver Eagles	F/A-18A	F-4S
VMFA-122	DC	Crusaders	F/A-18A	F-4S
VMFA-251	DW	Thunderbolts	F/A-18A	F-4S
VMFA-312	DR	Checkertails	F/A-18CN	F/A-18A
VMFA-333	DN	Shamrocks	F/A-18A	F-4S
VMFA-451	VM	Warlords	F/A-18A	F-4S
MCAS El Toro, Ca		MAW-3/MAG-11		
VMFA-314	VW	Black Knights	F/A-18A	F-4N
VMFA-323	WS	Death Rattlers	F/A-18A	F-4N
VMFA-531	EC	Grey Ghosts	F/A-18A	F-4N
VMFA(AW)-121	VK	Green Knights	F/A-18D	A-6E
VMFA(AW)-242	DT	Bats	F/A-18D	A-6E
VMFA(AW)-225	CE	Vikings	F/A-18D	–
VMFAT-101	SH	Sharpshooters	F/A-18A/B/C/D	F-4S
MCAS Kaneohe Bay, Hi		MAB-1/MAG-24		
VMFA-212	WD	Lancers	F/A-18C	F-4S
VMFA-232	WT	Red Devils	F/A-18C	F-4S
VMFA-235	DB	Death Angels	F/A-18C	F-4S
US MARINE CORPS/RESERVE				
MCAS El Toro, Ca		MAW-4/MAG-46		
VMFA-134	MF	Hawks	F/A-18A	F-4S
NAS Cecil Field, Fl		MAW-4/MAG-42, Det A		
VMFA-142	MB	Flying Gators	F/A-18A	A-4M
NAF Washington DC		MAW-4/MAG-41, Det A		
VMFA-321	MG	Black Barons	F/A-18A	F-4S
US NAVY				
NAF Atsugi, Japan				
VFA-192	NF	Golden Dragons	F/A-18C	F/A-18A
VFA-195	NF	Dam Busters	F/A-18C	F/A-18A
NAS Cecil Field, Fl				
VFA-15	AJ	Valions	F/A-18A	A-7E
VFA-37	AC	Bulls	F/A-18CN	A-7E

Unit	Code	Name	Type	Replacing/ Converted from
VFA-81	AA	Sunliners	F/A-18C	A-7E
VFA-82	AB	Marauders	F/A-18C	A-7E
VFA-83	AA	Rampagers	F/A-18C	A-7E
VFA-86	AB	Sidewinders	F/A-18C	A-7E
VFA-87	AJ	Golden Warriors	F/A-18A	A-7E
VFA-105	AC	Gunslingers	F/A-18CN	A-7E
VFA-106	AD	Gladiators	F/A-18A/B/C/D	–
VFA-131	AG	Wildcats	F/A-18CN	F/A-18A
VFA-132	AE	Privateers	F/A-18A	–
VFA-136	AG	Knight Hawks	F/A-18CN	F/A-18A
VFA-137	AE	Kestrels	F/A-18A	–
NAS Lemoore, Ca				
VFA-22	NH	Fighting Redcocks	F/A-18CN	A-7E
VFA-25	NK	Fist of the Fleet	F/A-18CN	F/A-18A
VFA-27	NL	Chargers	F/A-18A	A-7E
VFA-94	NH	Shrikes	F/A-18CN	A-7E
VFA-97	NL	Warhawks	F/A-18A	A-7E
VFA-113	NK	Stingers	F/A-18CN	F/A-18A
VFA-125	NJ	Rough Raiders	F/A-18A/B/C/D	–
VFA-146	NG	Blue Diamonds	F/A-18CN	A-7E
VFA-147	NG	Argonauts	F/A-18CN	A-7E
VFA-151	NM	Vigilantes	F/A-18A	F-4S
VFA-161	NM	Chargers	F/A-18A	F-4S
US NAVY/RESERVE				
VFA-203	AF	Blue Dolphins	F/A-18A	A-7E
VFA-204	AF	River Rattlers	F/A-18A	A-7E
VFA-303	ND	Golden Hawks	F/A-18A	A-7B
VFA-305	ND	Lobos	F/A-18A	A-7B
MISC UNITS				
VX-4	XF	Evaluators	F/A-18A, C, D	
VX-5	XE	Vampires	F/A-18A, C, D	
VAQ-34	–	Flashbacks	F/A-18A, B	
NATC*/SATD	SD	–	F/A-18A, C, D	
NSWC	–	Strike University	F/A-18A, B	
NWC*	–	–	F/A-18A, C, D	
NWEF*	–	–	F/A-18A	

Unit	Code	Name	Type	Replacing/ Converted from
PMTC*	–	–	F/A-18A, B, C	
TPS	–	–	F/A-18B	
USNFDT	–	Blue Angels	F/A-18A, B	
NASA	–	–	F/A-18A, B	
MACAIR	–	–	F/A-18	

NAS Point Mugu, Ca
NAS China Lake, Ca
NAS Lemoore, Ca: From NAS Point Mugu May 1991; 1st F/A-18 Jan 1992
NAS Patuxent River, Md: Naval Air Test Center/Strike Aircraft Test Directorate
NAS Fallon, NV: Naval Strike Warfare Center
NAS China Lake, Ca: Naval Weapons Center
Kirtland AFB, NM: Naval Weapons Evaluation Facility
NAS Point Mugu, Ca: Pacific Missile Test Center
NAS Patuxent River, Md: Test Pilot School
NAS Pensacola, Fl: US Navy Flight Demonstration Team
Edwards AFB, Ca: National Aeronautics & Space Administration
St Louis, Mo: McDonnell Aircraft Company

*Disestablished 1 January 1992 and consolidated within Naval Air Warfare Center (NAWC).

CVW	Carrier	Remarks
CVW-5	USS Independence	USS Midway
CVW-5	USS Independence	USS Midway
CVW-5	USS Theodore Roosevelt	
CVW-3	USS John F. Kennedy	
CVW-17	USS Saratoga	
CVW-1	USS America	
CVW-17	USS Saratoga	
CVW-1	USS America	
CVW-8	USS Theodore Roosevelt	
CVW-3	USS John F. Kennedy	
–	–	East Coast FRS
CVW-7	USS Dwight D. Eisenhower	
CVW-6	USS Forrestal	To be disest. Spring 1992
CVW-7	USS Dwight D. Eisenhower	
CVW-6	USS Forrestal	To CVW-2/USS Constellation
CVW-11	USS Abraham Lincoln	
CVW-14	USS Carl Vinson	From USS Midway
CVW-15	USS Kitty Hawk	
CVW-11	USS Abraham Lincoln	
CVW-15	USS Kitty Hawk	
CVW-14	USS Carl Vinson	From USS Midway
–	–	West Coast FRS
CVW-9	USS Nimitz	
CVW-9	USS Nimitz	
–	–	NAS Lamoore, Ca; to CVW-2 1992/USS Constellation
CVW-10	(USS Independence)	Disest. 1 April 1988
CVWR-20	–	NAS Cecil Field, Fl
CVWR-20	–	NAS New Orleans, La
CVWR-30	–	NAS Lemoore, Ca
CVWR-30	–	NAS Point Mugu, Ca
–	–	NAS Lamoore, Ca; to CVW-2 1992/USS Constellation

HORNETS ASSIGNED TO THE FSD PROGRAM

F1	160775	Flying qualities and flutter characteristics\
F2	160776	Performance and propulsion
F3	160777	Carrier trails
F4	160778	Envelope expansion and development
F5	160779	Weapons system development
F6	160780	High angle-of-attack development
T1	160781	Weapons system development
F7	160782	Weapons system development
F8	160783	Weapons system development
T2	160784	Aircraft availability and ease of maintainability
F9	160785	Aircraft availability and ease of maintainability

PROCUREMENT PROGRAM (USCM/USN)

Fiscal Year	Type	No. of aircraft	Serial number	Remarks
FY79	A/B	9	161213-217	B: 217
			161248-251	B: 249
FY80	A/B	25	161353-367	B: 354/57, 60
			161519-528	
FY81	A/B	60	161702/761	B: 704, 07, 11, 14, 19, 23, 27, 33, 40, 46
FY82	A/B	64	161924-987	B: 924, 32, 38, 43, 47
FY83	A/B	84	162394-477	B: 402, 08, 13, 19, 27
FY84	A/B	84	162826-909	B: 836, 42, 50, 57, 64, 70, 76, 85
FY85	A/B	84	163092-175	B: 104, 10, 15, 23
FY86	C/D	84	163427/510	D: 434, 36, 41, 45, 47, 52, 54, 57, 60, 64, 68, 72, 74, 79, 82, 86, 88, 92, 97, 500, 01, 07,10
FY87	C/D	84	163699-782	D: 700, 07, 20, 34, 49, 63, 71, 78
FY88	C/D	84	163985-4068	D: 986, 89, 91, 94, 97, 001, 05, 09,11, 11, 14, 17, 19, 22, 24, 26, 28, 32, 35, 38, 40, 43, 46, 49, 51, 53, 56, 58, 61, 64, 68
FY89	C/D	84	164196-279	D: 196, 98, 203, 07, 11, 16, 19, 24, 28, 33, 37, 41, 45, 49, 54, 59, 63, 67, 72, 79
FY90	C/D	66	**164627-692**	D: 649/53, 56, 59, 62, 65, 67, 70, 72, 74, 77, 79, 83, 85, 88, 90, 92
FY91	C/D	48	164693-740	D: 694, 99, 702, 05, 11, 14, 17, 23, 26, 29, 35, 38
FY92	C/D	48	164865-912	D: 866, 69, 73, 76, 80, 83, 86, 89, 93, 97, 901, 04, 07, 10
FY93	C/D	48		
FY94	C/D	54		
FY95	C/D	54		
FY96	C/D	54		

PROCUREMENT PROGRAM (CANADA)   FY81/FY86

CF-18A   188701-798 (98)
CF-18B   188901-940 (40)

PROCUREMENT PROGRAM (AUSTRALIA)   FY83/FY87

F/A-18A   A21-1/57 (57)
F/A-18B   A21-101/118 (18)

PROCUREMENT PROGRAM (SPAIN)   FY84/FY88

EF-18A   C.15-13/72 (60)
EF-18B   CE.15-1/12 (12)

PROCUREMENT PROGRAM (KUWAIT)   FY90/FY91

F/A-18C   401-432 (32)
F/A-18D   441-448 (8)

AUSTRALIA
(all units fly both F/A-18A and F/A-18B aircraft)

3 Squadron*		Williamtown, NSW	Mirage III O
75 Squadron		Tindal, NT	Mirage III O/OD
77 Squadron*	Magpie	Williamtown, NSW	Mirage IIi O/OD
2 OCU*	Tiger	Williamtown, NSW	Mirage III O/OD

*Assigned to No 81 Fighter Wing

CANADA
(all units fly both CF-18A and CF-18B aircraft)

409 Squadron (TF)*	Nighthawk	Baden-Söllingen, FRG	CF-101B/F
410 Squadron (TFT)	Cougar	Cold Lake, Alberta	CF-101B/F
416 Squadron (TF)	Lynx	Cold Lake, Alberta	CF-101B/F
421 Squadron (TF)**	Red Indian	Baden-Söllingen, FRG	CF-104D/G
425 Squadron (TF)	Alouette	Bagotville, Quebec	CF-101B/F
433 Squadron (TF)	Porcupine	Bagotville, Quebec	CF-5A/D
439 Squadron (TF)**	Tiger	Baden-Söllingen, FRG	CF-104D/G
441 Squadron (TF)	Silver Fox	Cold Lake, Alberta	CF-104D/G
Aircraft Engineering Test Establishment (AETE)		Cold Lake, Alberta	–

*Disbanded 25 June 1991
**Assigned to No 4 Fighter Wing; to return to Canada by 1994

SPAIN
(all units fly both EF-18A and EF-18B aircraft)

121 Squadron*	Poker	Torrejon	F-4C
122 Squadron*	Tenis	Torrejon	F-4C
151 Squadron**	Ebro	Zaragoza	–
152 Squadron**	Marte	Zaragoza	–

*Assigned to Ala de Caza 12
**Assigned to Ala de Caza 15